Bevilacqua

CONTENTS

PREFACE

Louisiana has always shown contemporary art. And we have always done so in an interplay with both the sister arts and the great classic exhibitions. The most important thing for a museum like Louisiana is to add to knowledge and understanding of how all our cultural gestures both spread like ripples in the water and draw on events and insights that have gone before, irrespective of whether anyone can map out their history, of whether we can connect the phenomena like pieces in a jigsaw puzzle.

Louisiana tries not to present contemporary art to the few and classic modernism to the many: we treat both in the belief that they can all still contribute to human self-understanding and our understanding of the world. And the assumption is, by the way, that all art has once been contemporary.

Michael Bevilacqua's exhibition at Louisiana is the first in a series of seven exhibitions that the museum is doing over the next two and a half years under the label *Louisiana Contemporary*. The exhibitions will be independent profilings of important younger artists who have demonstrated a serious and sincere interest in their field. Michael Bevilacqua is just such an artist. Although he expresses himself in a formal language and with an iconography that is intensely of today, his painting is far more complex than it looks on the surface. And it is not least these emerging qualities in the expression and its determined administration that have fascinated Louisiana, which already acquired a work by Bevilacqua in 2004.

With Bevilacqua at Louisiana – incidentally the artist's first museum exhibition – the institution is both lining up for a new and looking back to a long-standing confrontation with American art – a confrontation that in the Danish context has been the sole preserve of the museum in Humlebæk. We have Warhol, Rauschenberg, Dine and Lichtenstein in the collection, and in recent years we have shown both Warhol and Lichtenstein in large one-man exhibitions. At the same time Bevilacqua's exhibition itself lines up in many respects with the artificial pictorial world of a Thomas Demand and the virtuosity of a Doug Aitken – two artists Louisiana has also recently presented to the Scandinavian public.

First and foremost I would like to thank the artist for his fine cooperation, and for his involvement in and enthusiasm for this project. Our warmest thanks too to the galleries involved – Galleri Faurschou, Deitch Projects and Mitchell-Innes & Nash, who have all provided support for the realization of this catalogue. Thanks to the writers Michael Juul Holm and Meghan Dailey and to the designer of this book Michael Jensen, as well as the coordinator of the exhibition Anna-Maria Lund, and to Jannie Haagemann from Galleri Faurschou in Copenhagen, who has been of unfailing assistance in the process.

Finally, our great gratitude to the lenders – institutional as well as private – who have made the exhibition possible: the Astrup Fearnley Collection, Meredith and Bryan Verona, the Dallas Museum of Art, the Dakis Joannu Collection, Neuberger Berman, the Neumann Family Collection, and Norman Dubrow. Thanks also to Michael Danoff, Jeffrey Deitch, Luise and Jens Faurschou, Lucy Mitchell-Innes, Robert Grossman, Meghan Coleman, Vicki and Kent Logan, Maria and Jesper Stieler, Dakis Joannou, Peter Bennedsen, the Speyer Family Collection and Chad Gravelle of Gravelle Race Cars.

Last but not least, I would like to thank DONG, the principal sponsor of Louisiana's exhibitions in 2000-2005, and especially Nykredit, who have taken on the sponsorship of Louisiana Contemporary in 2005 and 2006.

Poul Erik Tøjner,
Director,
Louisiana Museum of Modern Art

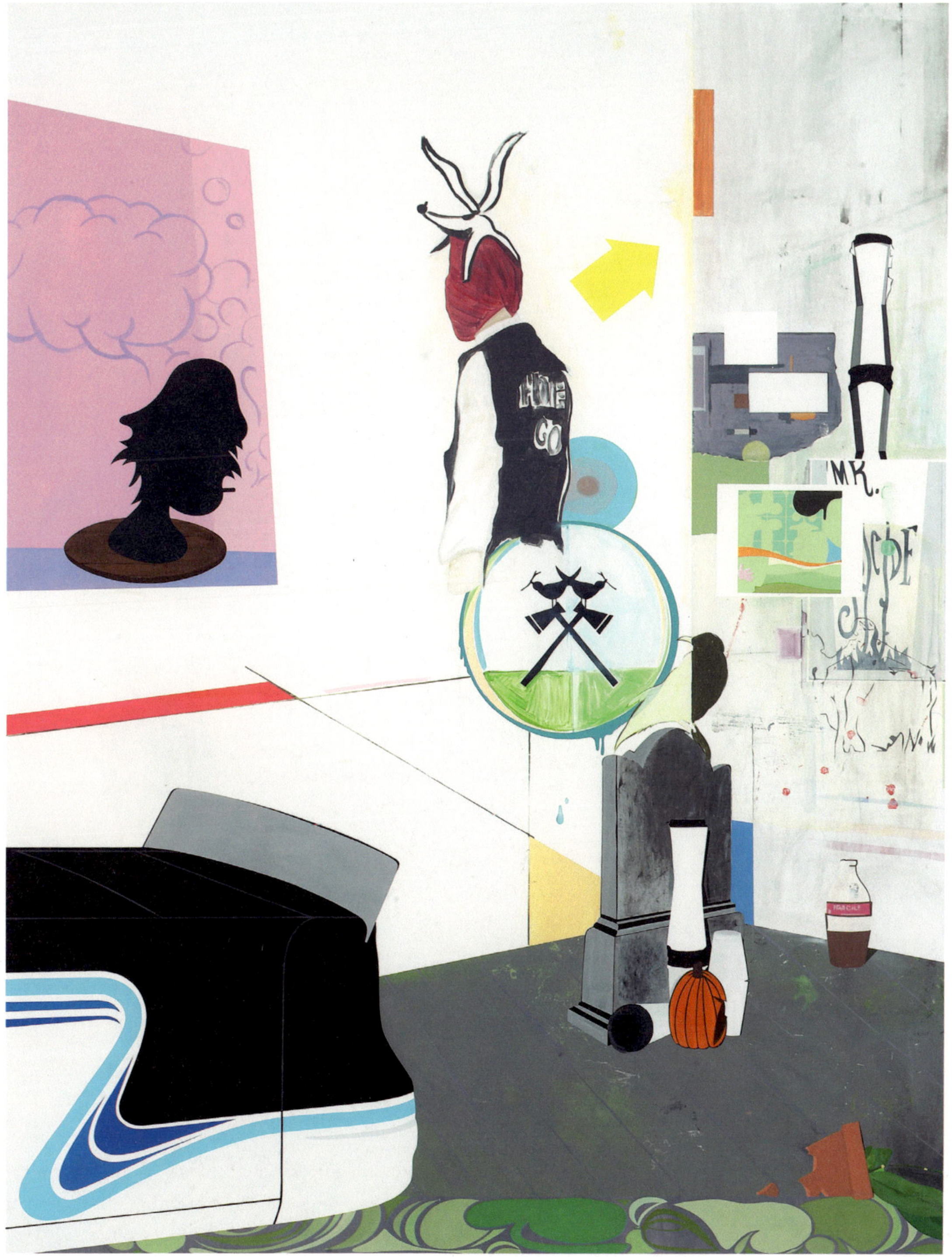

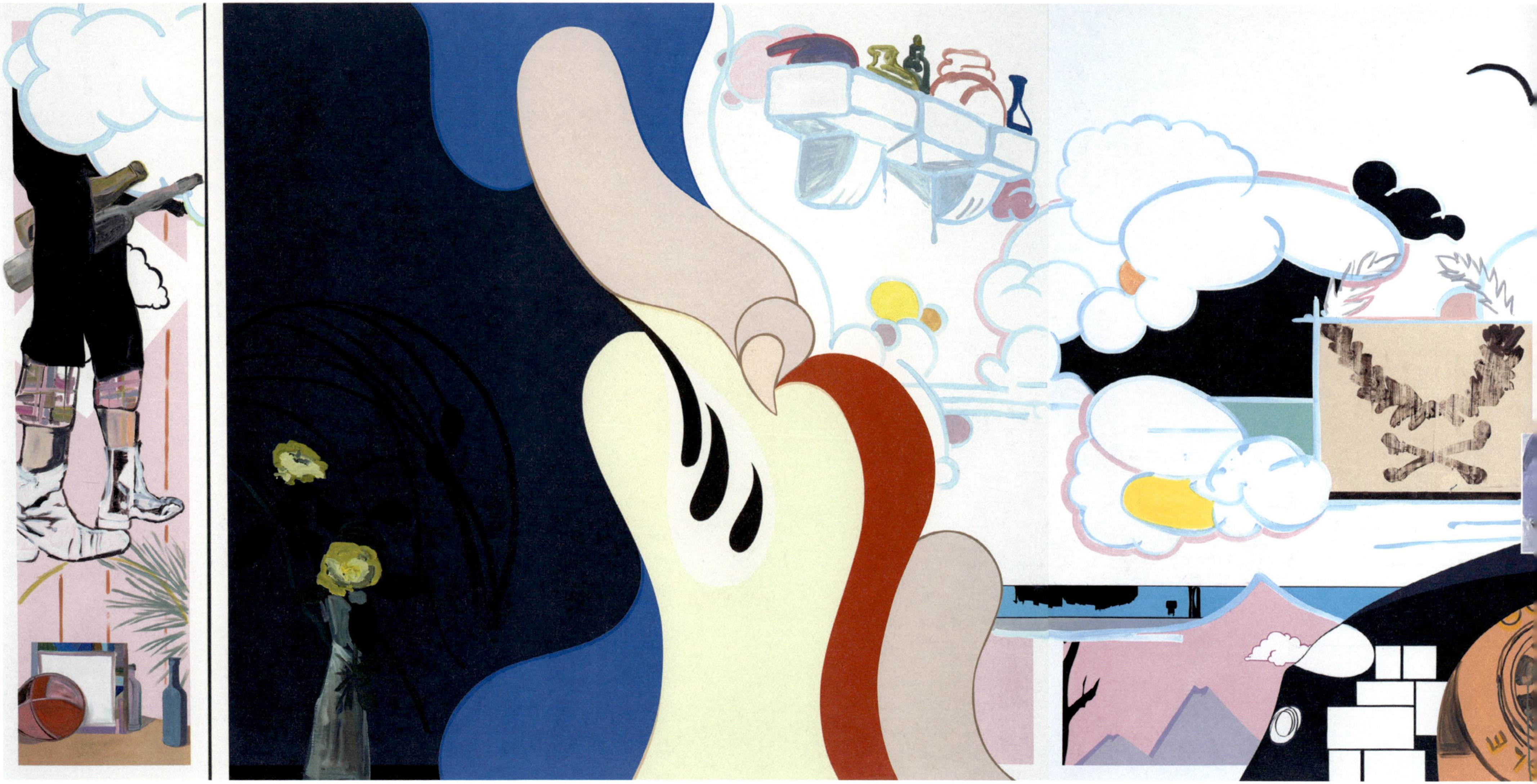

Surface to Air. 2004

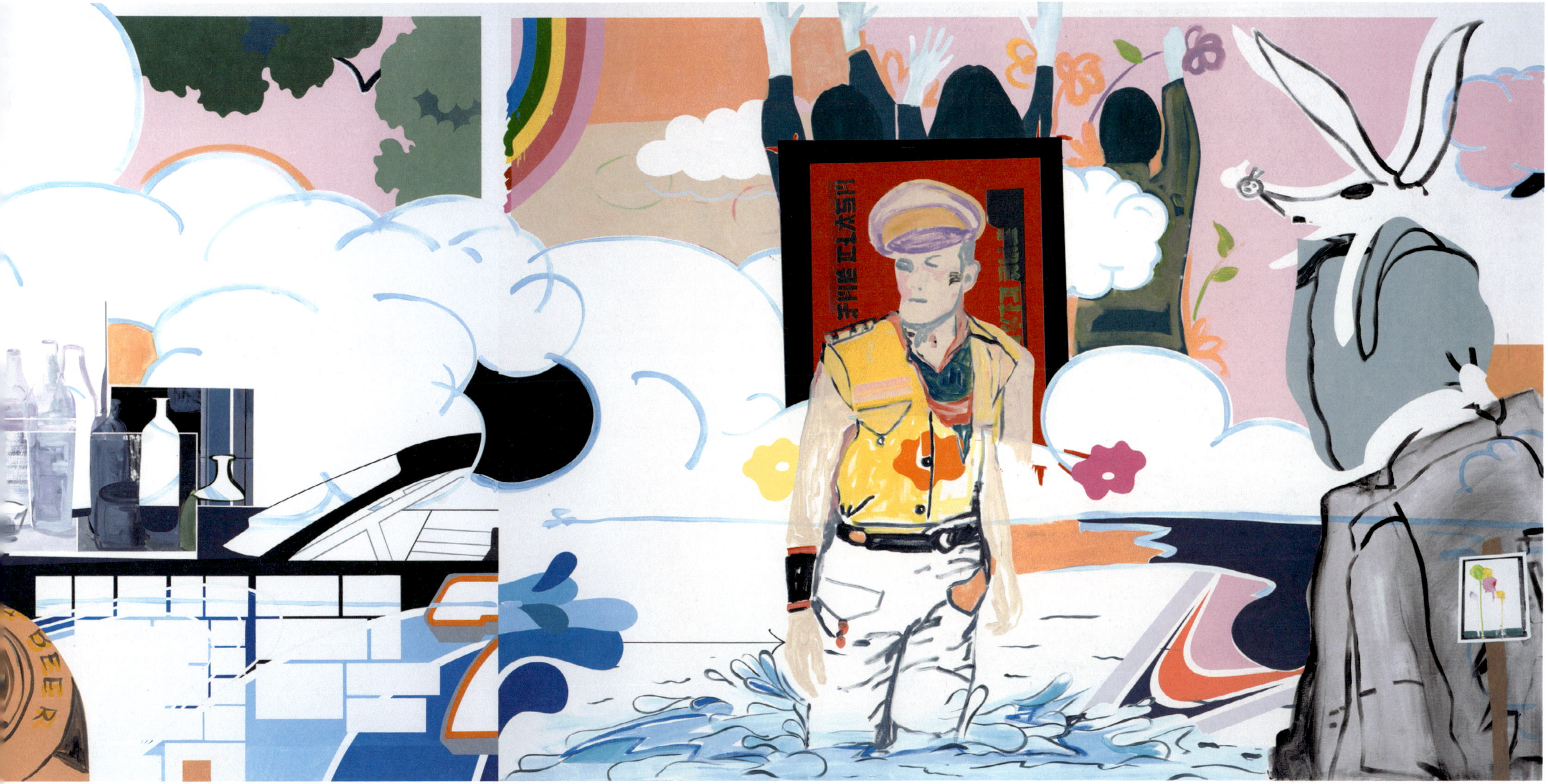
BEER

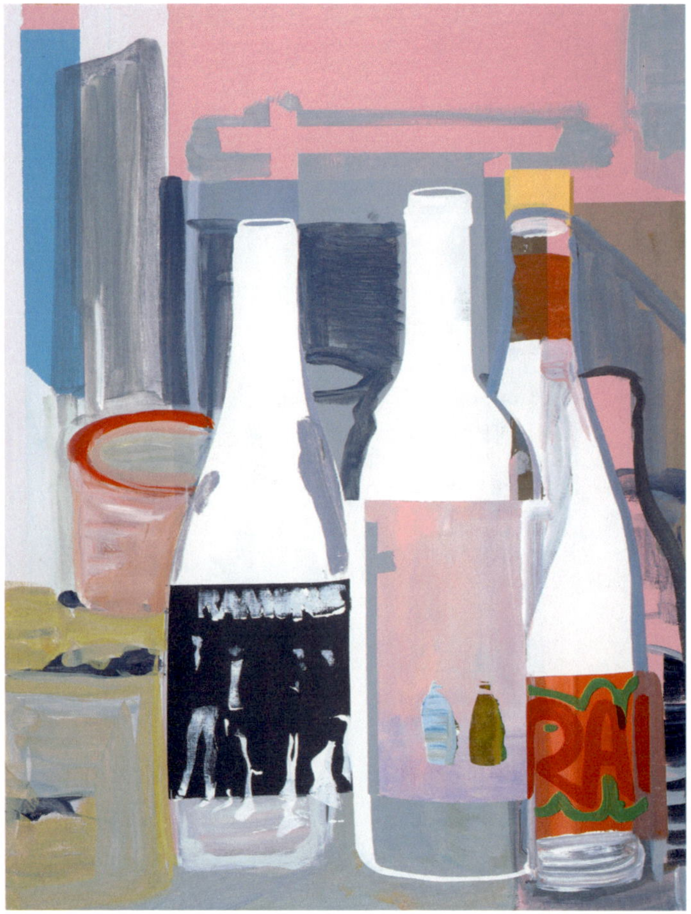

Daytime Dilemma (Dangers of Love). 2005

Inside Looking Out. 2004

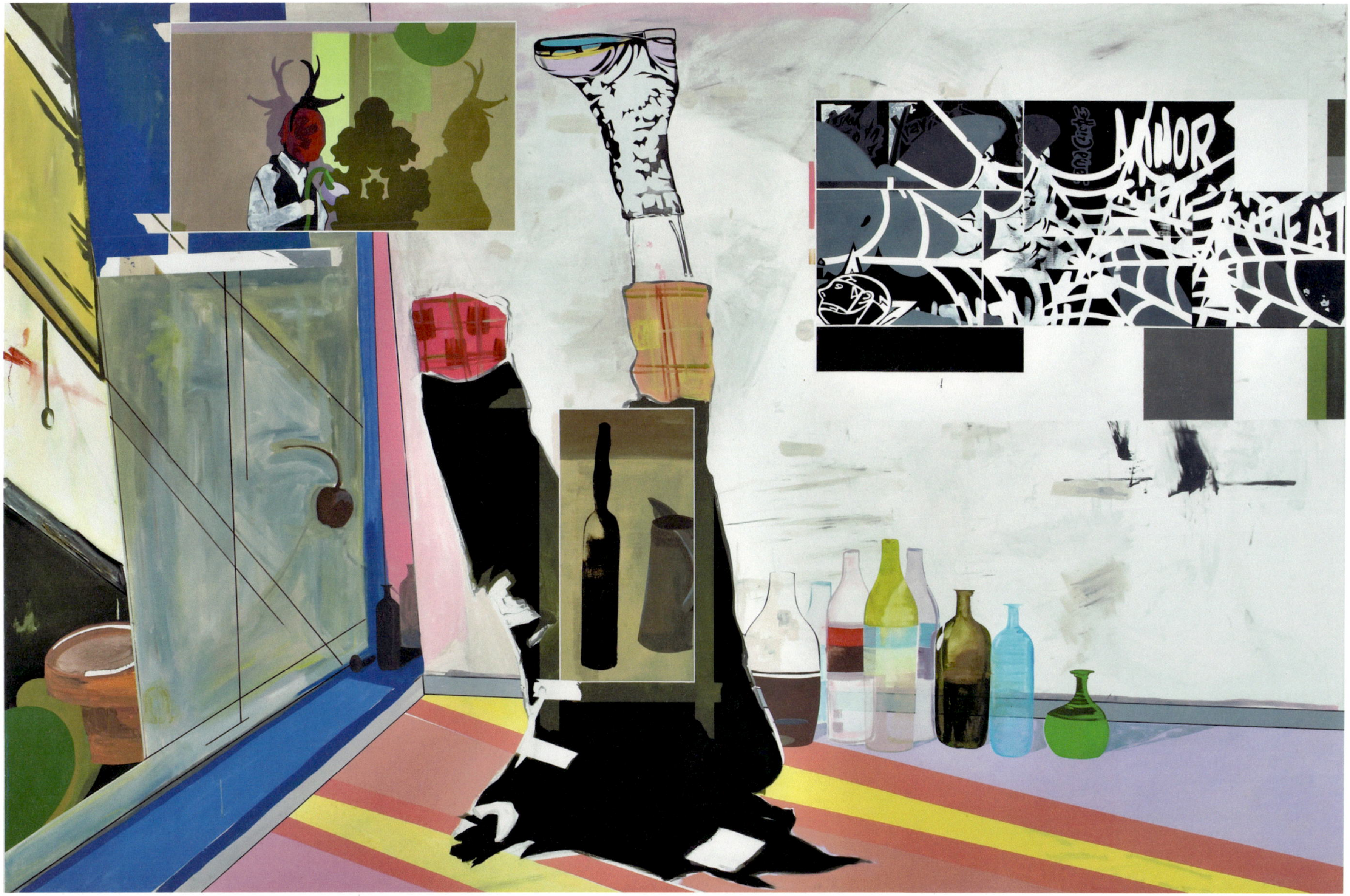
MINOR

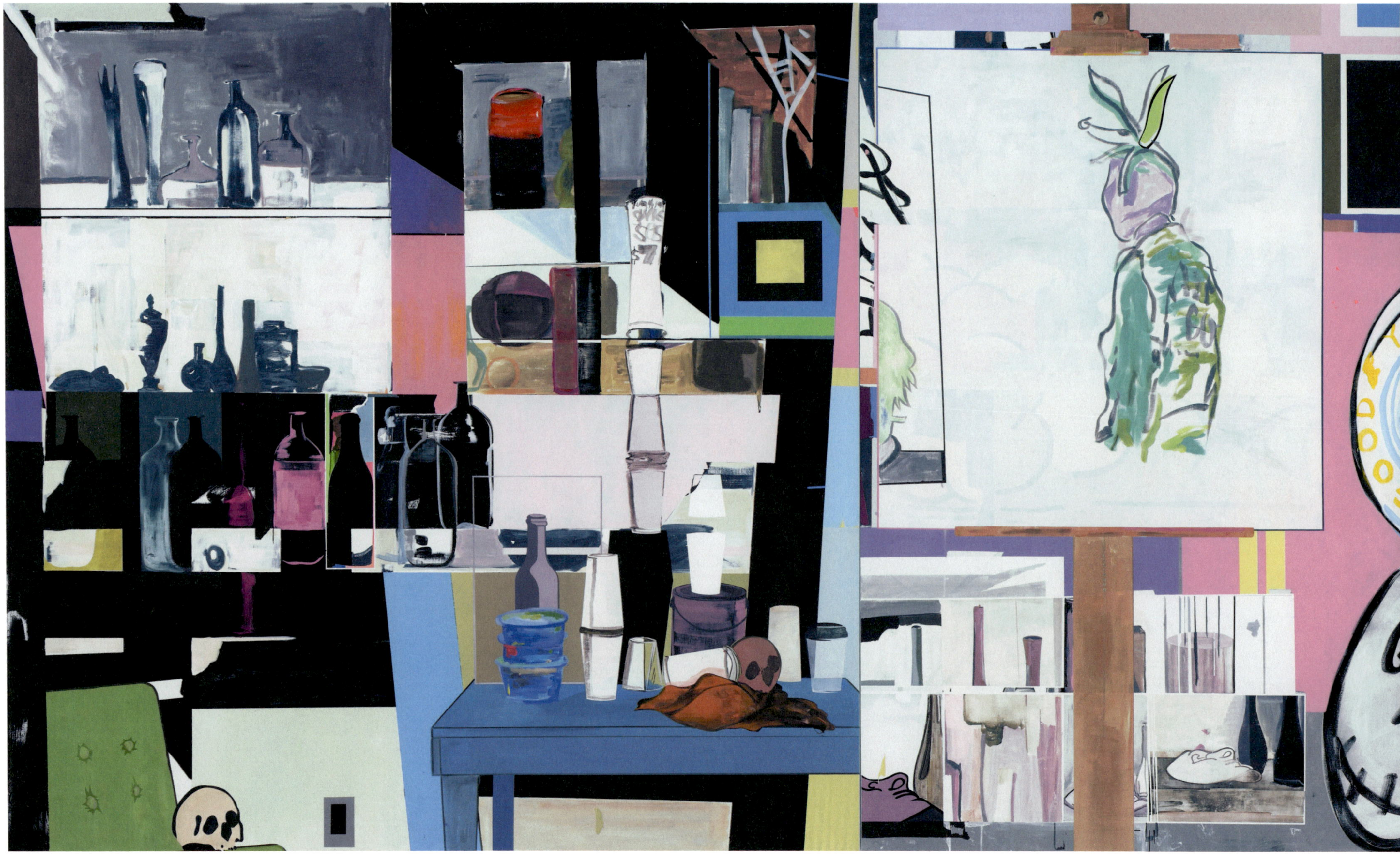

Black Studio. 2004

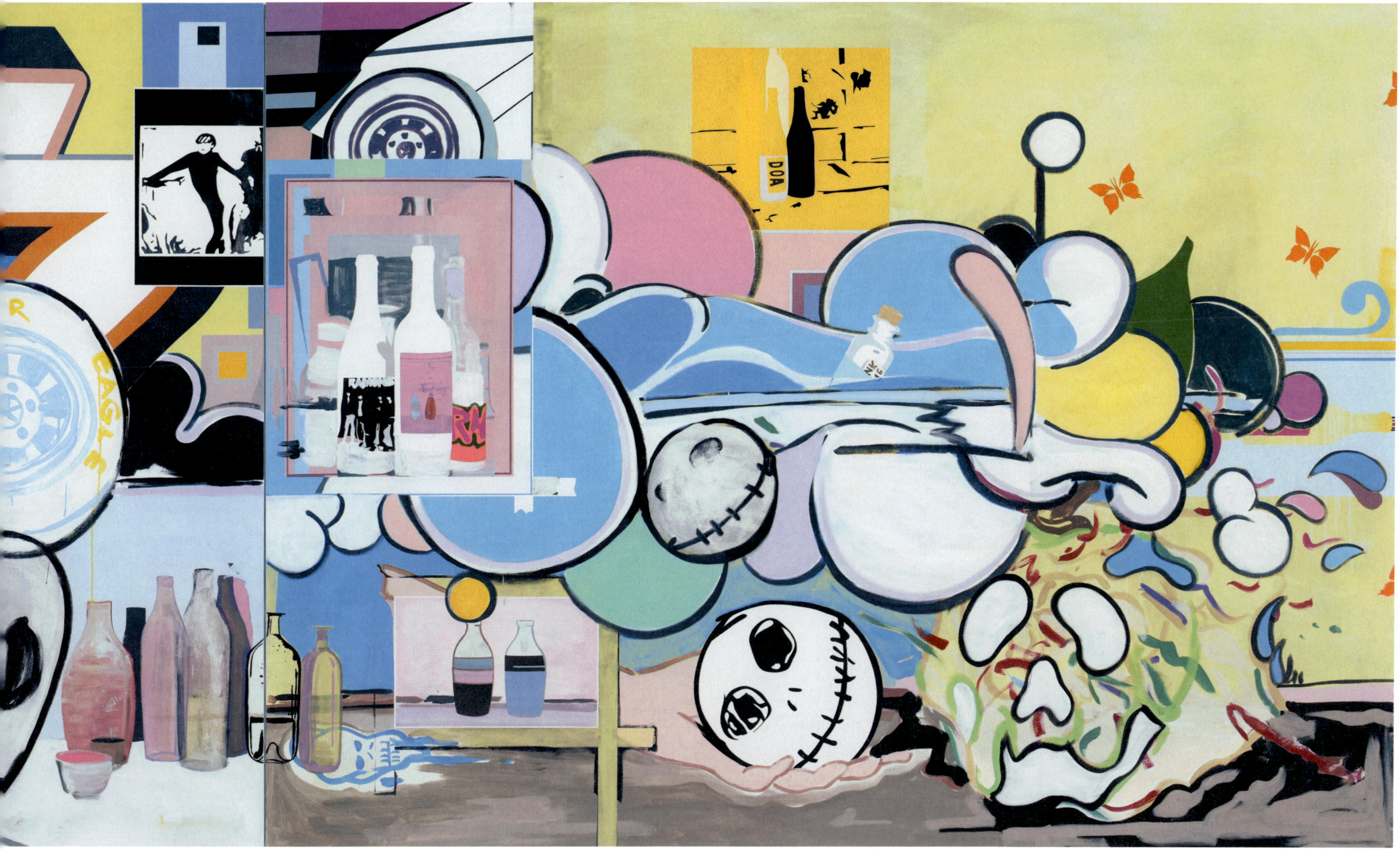
DOA

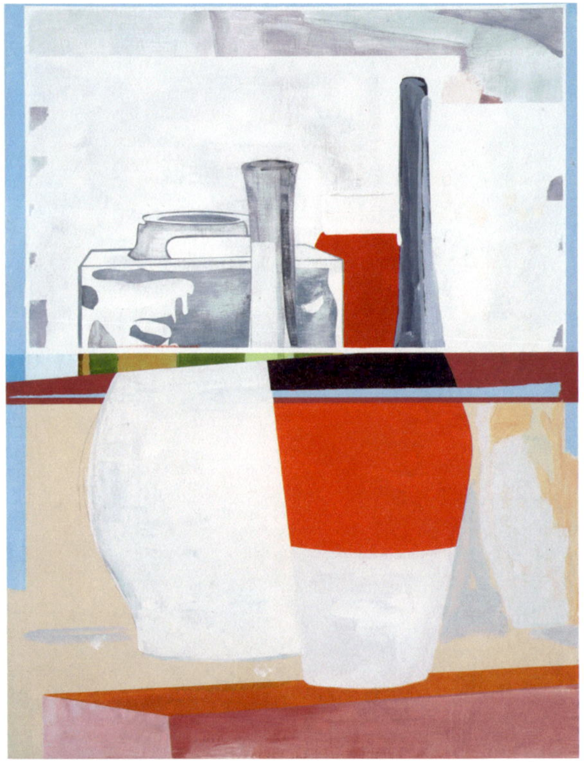

Psypotica. 2004

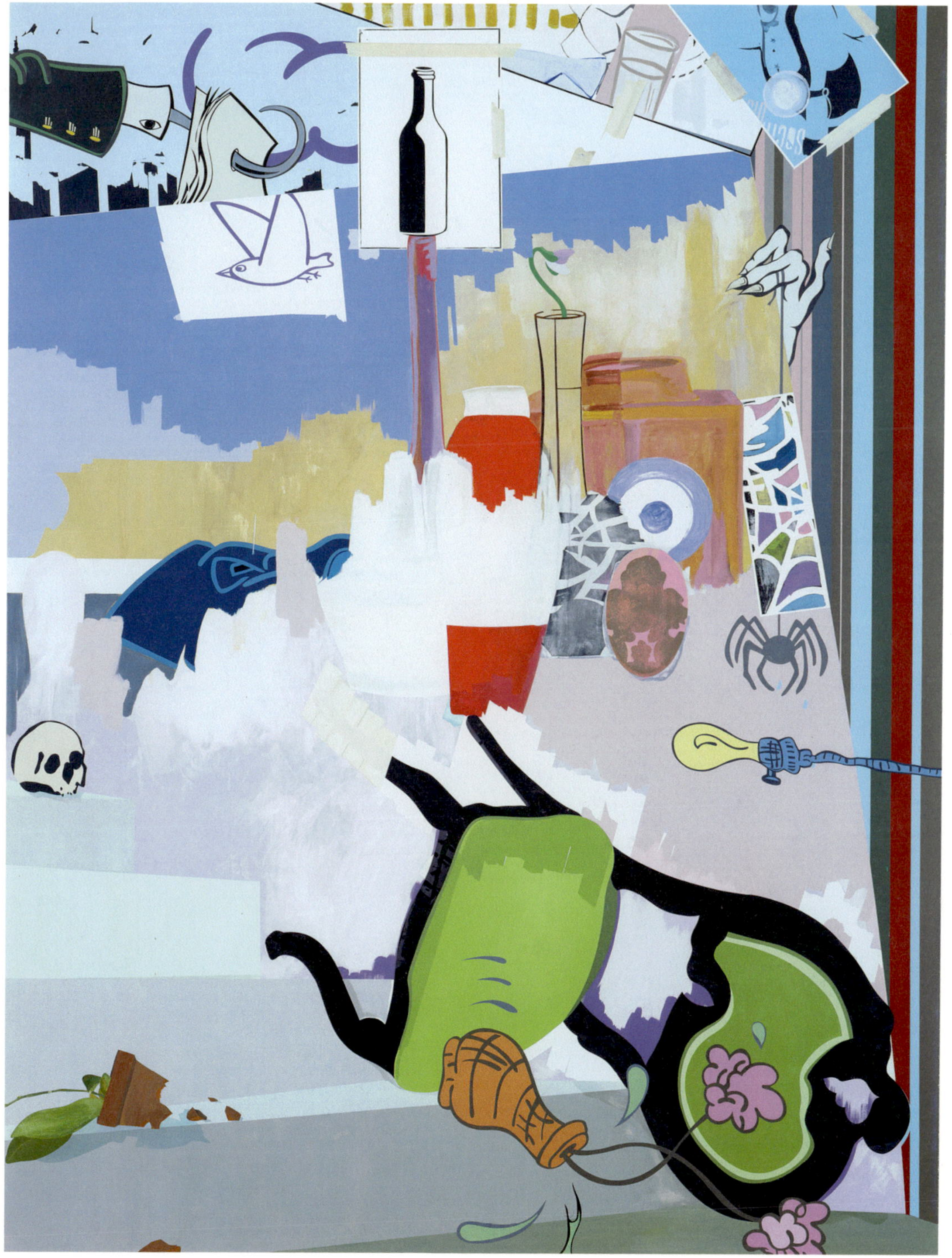

The Mystery Spot. 2004

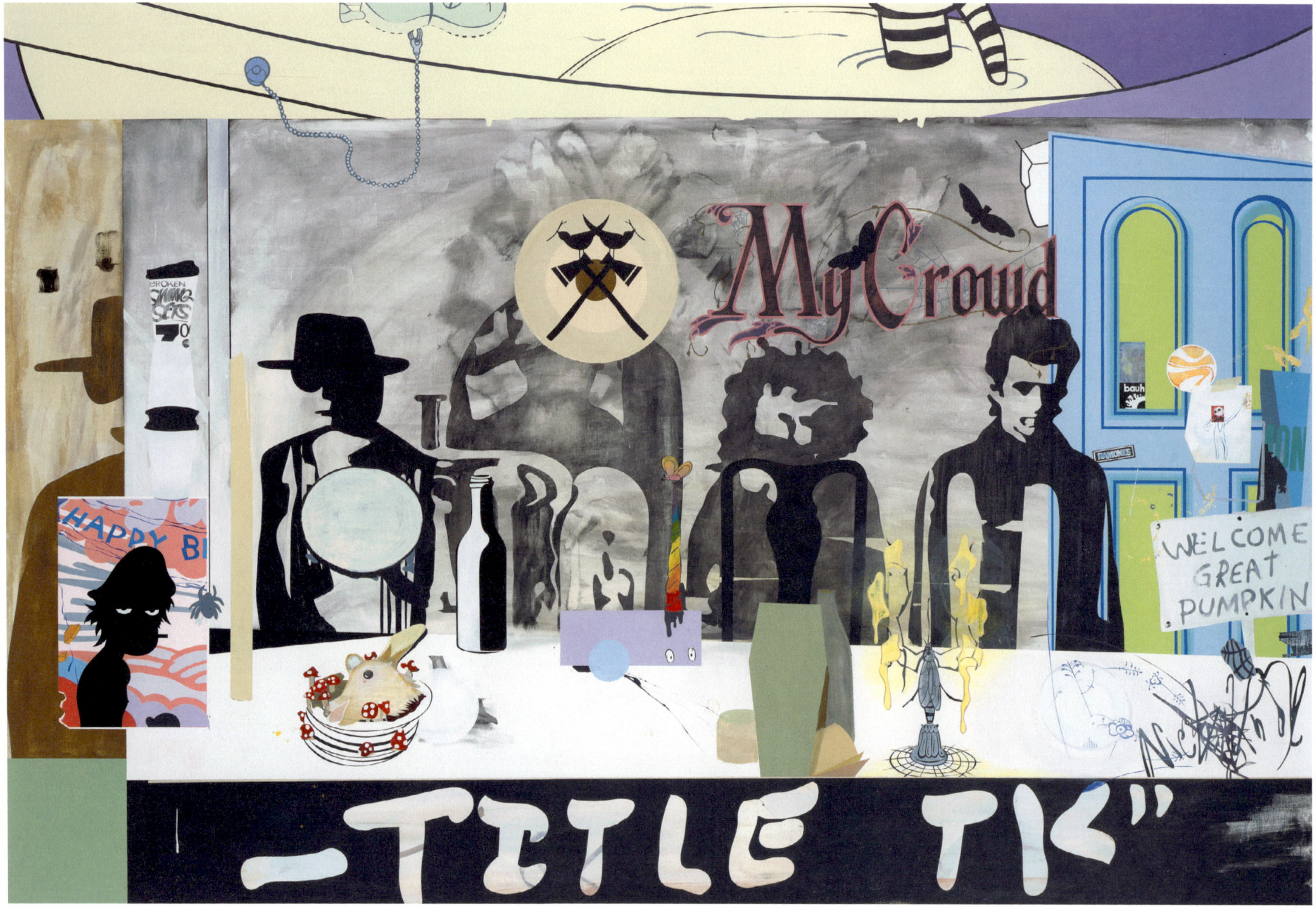
MyCrowd
WELCOME
GREAT
PUMPKIN
HAPPY BI
TITLE TIK"

Beyond and Back, 2004

DEAR DIARY: MICHAEL BEVILACQUA'S POP SUBJECTIVE / MEGHAN DAILEY

A few years ago, Michael Bevilacqua took a trip to Paris. During his stay, he visited a hybrid boutique/gallery called Surface to Air that features what the proprietors call "products of creativity" – music, fashion, and art. Its eclecticism immediately appealed to Bevilacqua, whose paintings are built on a similar underlying concept: pull together what moves you the most from your daily experience and synthesize the mix into a unified whole. Not long afterward, he made a painting and titled it *Surface to Air* (2004).

That ambitious work makes reference to the artist's Paris journey and more. Bevilacqua considers *Surface to Air* to be a kind of summation of his feelings from the last few years and it casts a wide net. It embodies many of the themes that have long occupied him, such as music, popular culture, and references to art making. This expansive three-panel work takes us from the ground (there is a figure standing in water and a black race car emblazoned with the number 7) to the atmosphere (the airy clouds are based on sketches he made looking out an airplane window on a trip to Greece). In some ways it's about revisiting old ideas and making them new. The arrangement of bottles refers back to the formal exercises he completed in a still-life course as a college student. That was the only painting class he ever took. Upon rediscovering the old canvases in his parents' garage, he decided to revisit the traditional theme as a way of proving to himself how far he has come as an artist.

Replete with such personal references, *Surface to Air* also maintains the diaristic quality that informs all of his enterprise: call it Autobiographical Pop. No matter how recognizable an image may be, it always has some personal significance for Bevilacqua. "Everything about my work is very specific, nothing is random," he says. Whether it is a Louis Vuitton logo, the name of a punk-rock band, the face of a cartoon character, or an abstract passage of color, each element in his art relates to his life: his family, his personal history, his passions, what his kids are watching on TV, where he travels, his own working process.

Music is crucial to that process – he cannot work in his studio without listening to music. Looking at a selection of his works reveals what's on the stereo. Mostly it's bands from the decade of the artist's youth, the 1980s: Gang of Four, the Ramones, Surf Punks, as well as more recent groups like Air and Stereolab. In *Surface to Air*, the allusion may be veiled, but it is present. The figure in military dress represents punk-rock pioneer Joe Strummer, the late singer and guitarist of The Clash, one of Bevilacqua's favorite bands for as long as he can remember.

Recontextualization of the everyday

While *Surface to Air* contains familiar tropes, it also indicates a shift in Bevilacqua's practice. Formally, it demonstrates a looser, more painterly and abstract style that he has developed over the past few years. This is a move away from the harder-edged graphic style that characterized his earlier work, and except for the laurel wreath-and-crossbones logo of the Surface to Air store that hovers in the center panel, the composition is conspicuously free of the multiple, overlapping logos that have become so common in Bevilacqua's art. He has purposely obliterated the logos, he says, because he was frustrated that viewers did not seem to understand that those insignia were not merely ends to themselves, but also formal vehicles–they functioned as things to be painted.

Herein lies one of the problematic aspects of his work and a potential dilemma of any work that falls under the rubric of Pop: its hyper-legibility renders it deceptively simple. Bevilacqua's works are anything but. For all of their smoothness – they are saturated more than gestural – the works are very painterly in their conception and are painstakingly executed in a time-consuming process that constantly evolves. Bevilacqua's works are not just assortments of logos or colorful, random panoplies of media culture; he may be painting youth culture, but he's approaching it with an experienced hand and an educated eye.

The full force of his skills as a painter will be in view at the Louisiana Museum, where three large-scale works will be shown together: *Under the Influence: Geek USA*, *Highly Evolved* (both 2004), and *Busy, Busy, Sunny Day* (2003). Each has been exhibited separately, but Bevilacqua considers them a single work, and they will be installed contiguously for the first time.

By virtue of its scale and juxtaposition of multiple images, that panorama brings to mind one of the icons of Pop art, James Rosenquist's enormous wraparound painting *F-111*, from 1964-65. In its complex visual layering, and recontextualization of the everyday into the realm of art, it's hard not to consider Bevilacqua's work in the lineage of 1960s Pop art and Rosenquist in particular.

Automotive Distraction II. 2004

From L.A. to NYC

But Bevilacqua also takes inspiration from the later, looser, and more personal California variants of the genre (sometimes the works combine the sensibilities and iconography of both coasts, fittingly for a Californian transplanted to New York). His interest in cars, for example, recalls the L.A. gambit of artists such as Billy Al Bengston. During the 1960s Bengston elevated car customizing to the level of gallery art with his use of materials like liquid wax and spray paint. While he was growing up, Bevilacqua spent a lot of time with a friend whose family was involved in racing cars and has remained fascinated by the look of these vehicles. In 2004, he exhibited a stock car alongside his paintings, covering with stickers depicting details of his own works and other images. The car body became a metaphor for the artist himself: it was made in California, but "completed" in New York.

He is also aware of the wry self-deprecation and dark humor of artists like Raymond Pettibon, Mike Kelley, and Jim Shaw, whose work he first encountered while he was living in Los Angeles in the 1980s. Bevilacqua was inspired by their lowbrow sources – comic books, pulp novels, and album covers – and their generally anti-establishment posture. This self-effacing stance is evident in Bevilacqua's self-portraits, which are often oblique and inserted among a welter of other images. Recently, he has begun to depict himself as a somnambulist, the unconscious performer of actions. This figure's head is completely covered, almost as if by bandages. More a gestalt than a likeness, this figure is the perfect non-logo for Bevilacqua to signify his presence. In a sea of signs and signifiers, an endless parade of brand names, color choices and 10,000 songs on the Ipod, the self is always the anchor.

Meghan Dailey (b. 1970) is a critic and editor living in Brooklyn, New York. She writes frequently about contemporary art and has contributed to *Artforum*, *Parkett*, and many other publications.

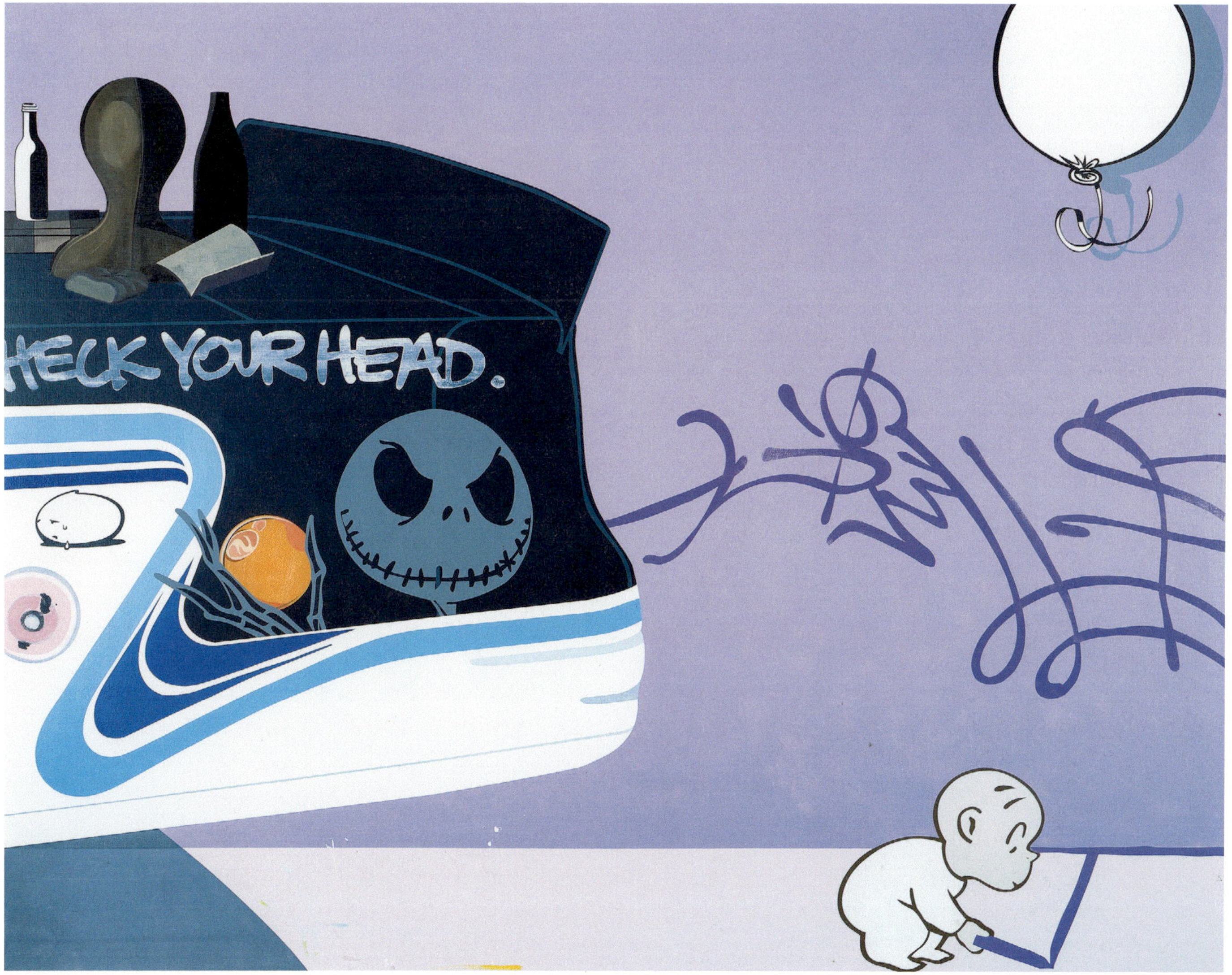
HECK YOUR HEAD.

Busy, Busy Sunny Day. 2003

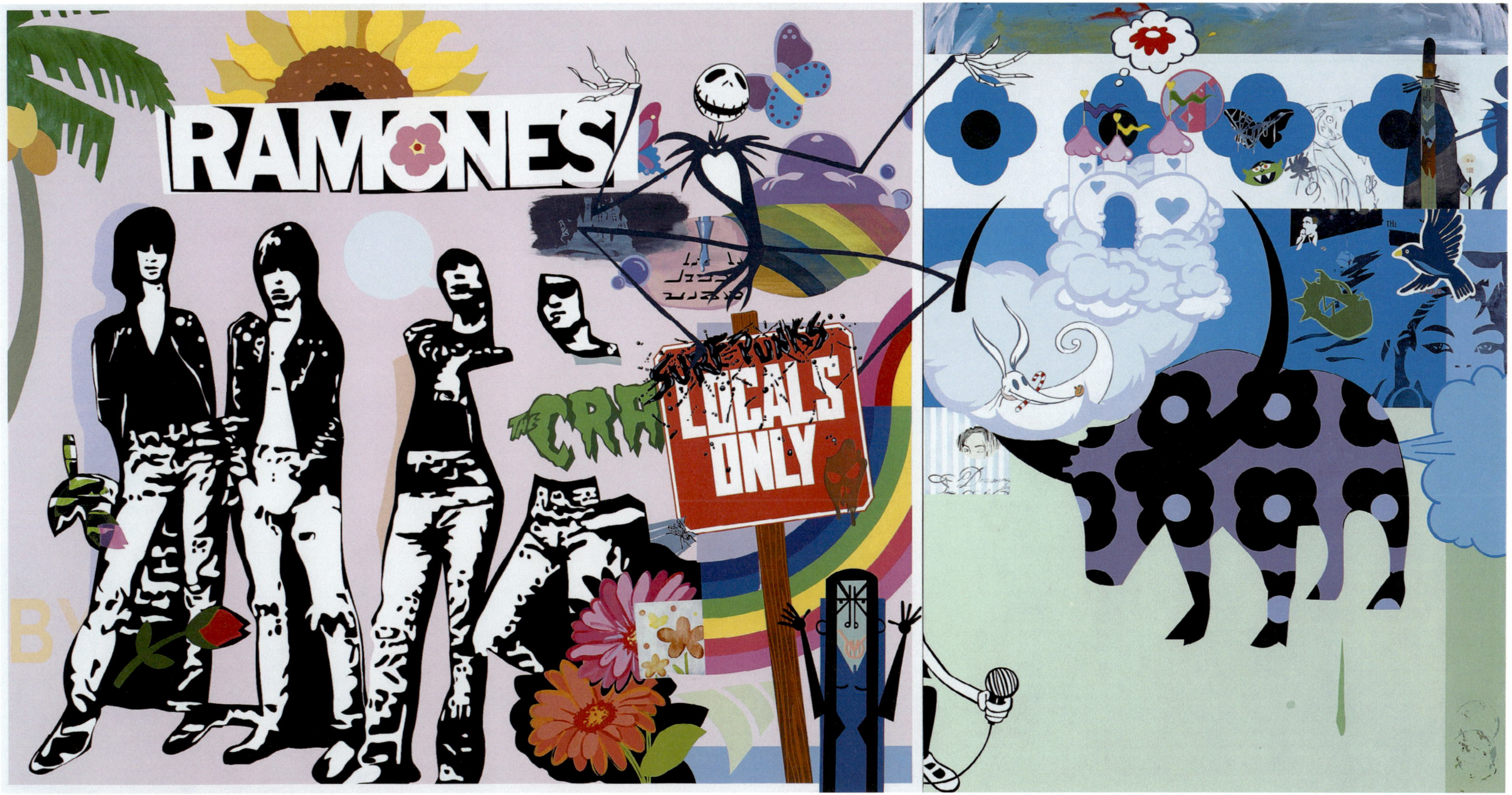
RAMONES
LOCALS ONLY

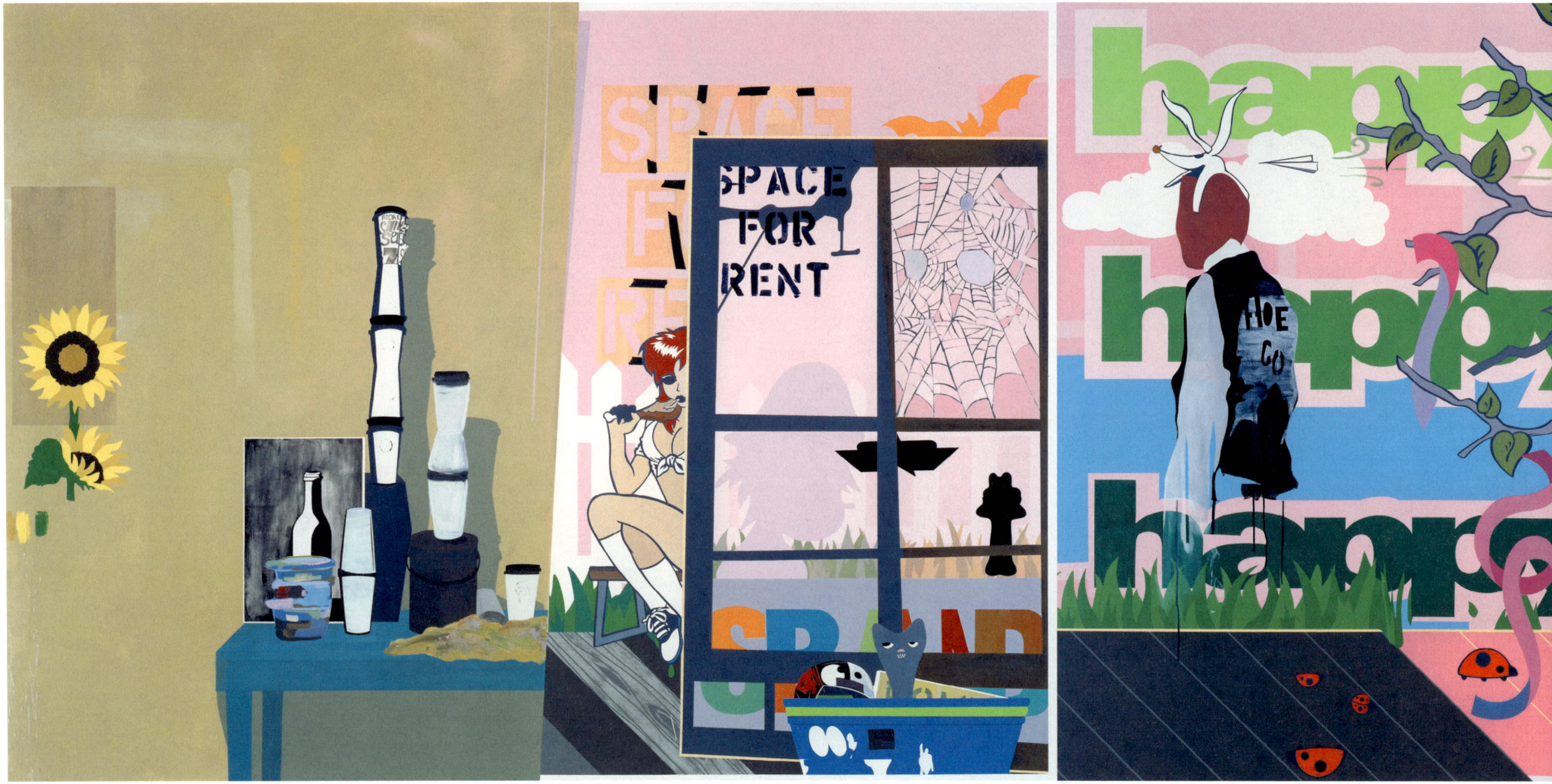

Highly Evolved. 2004

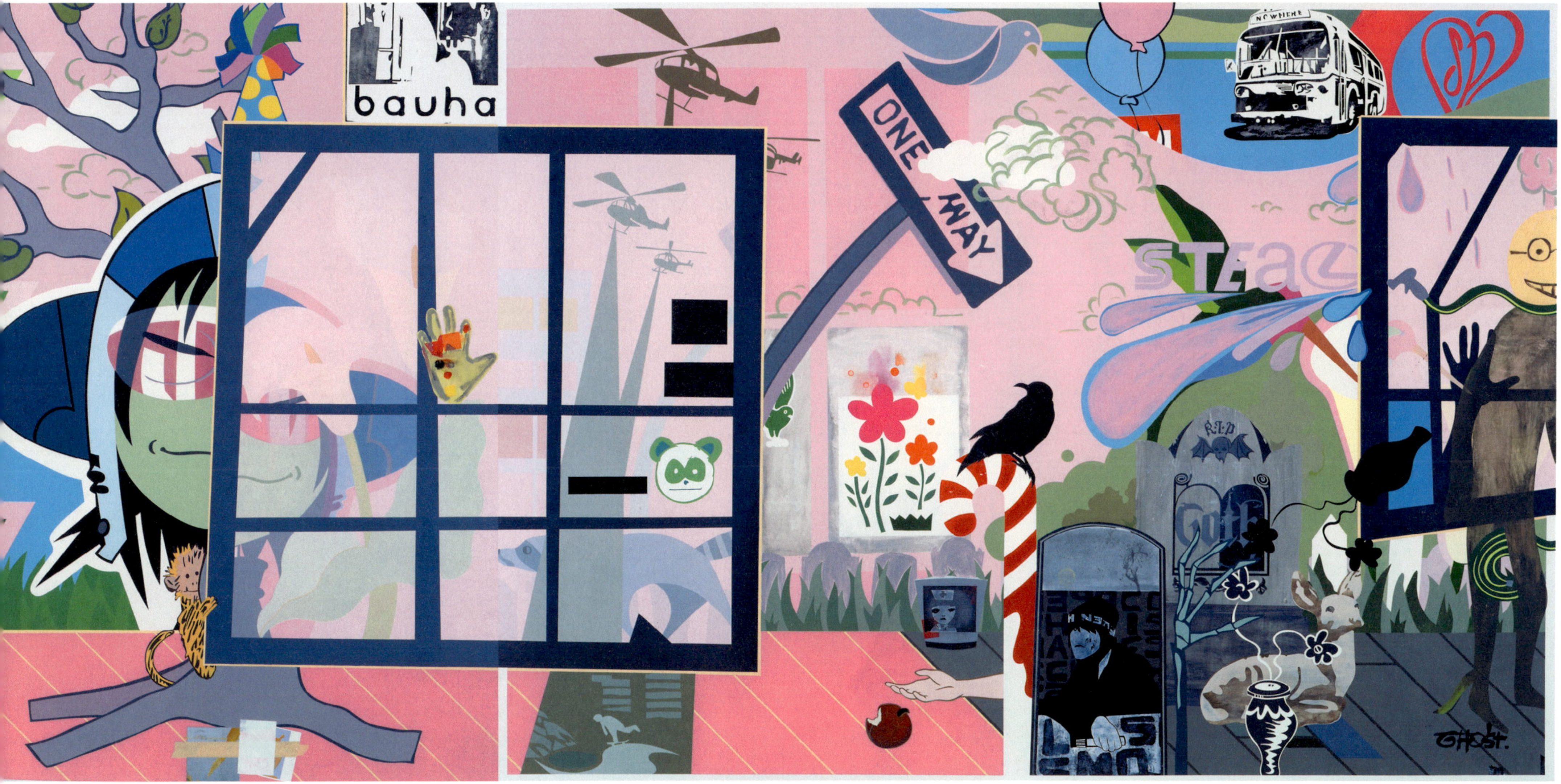
bauha
ONE WAY
GHOST.

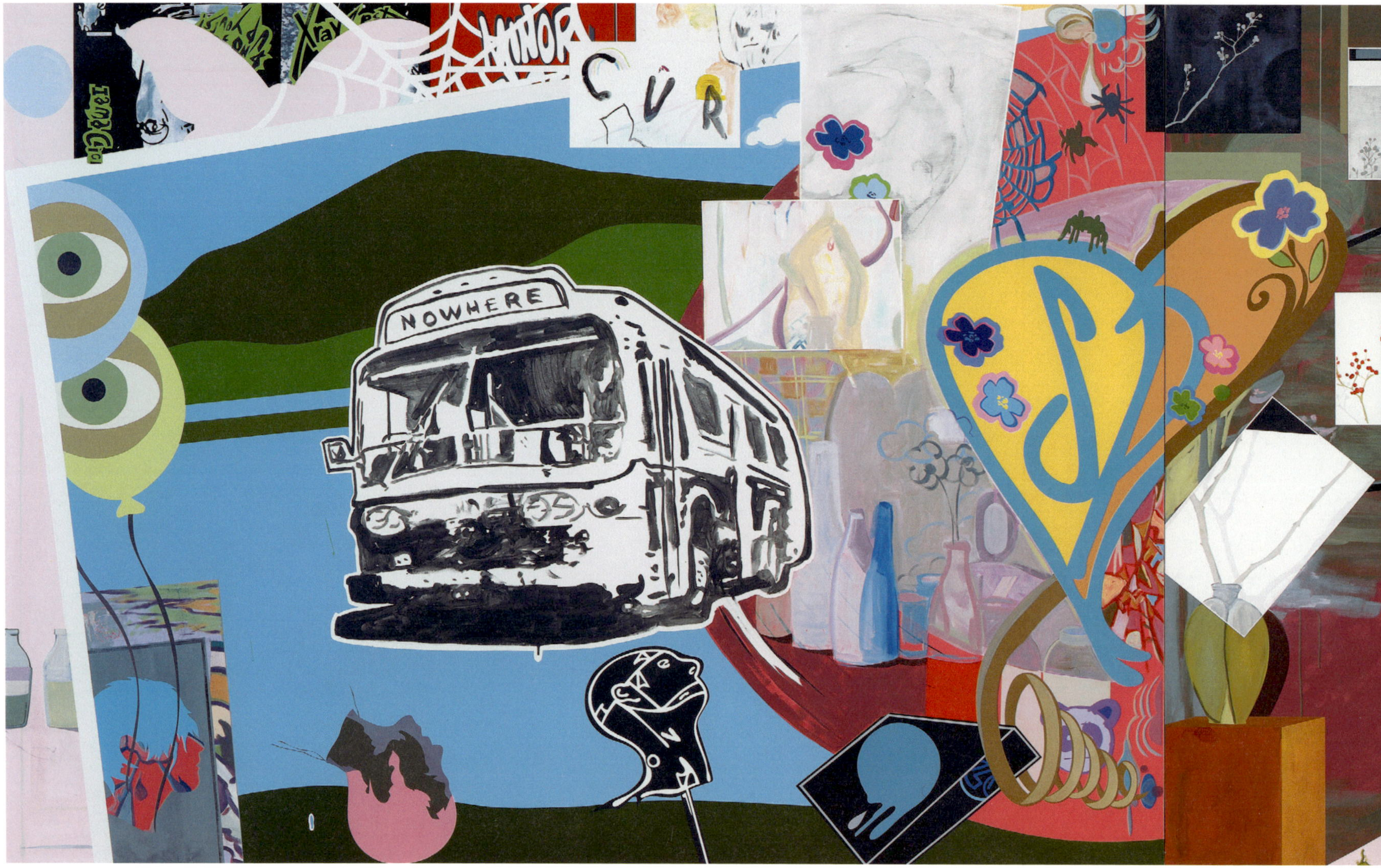

Drawing Under the Influence: Geek USA. 2004

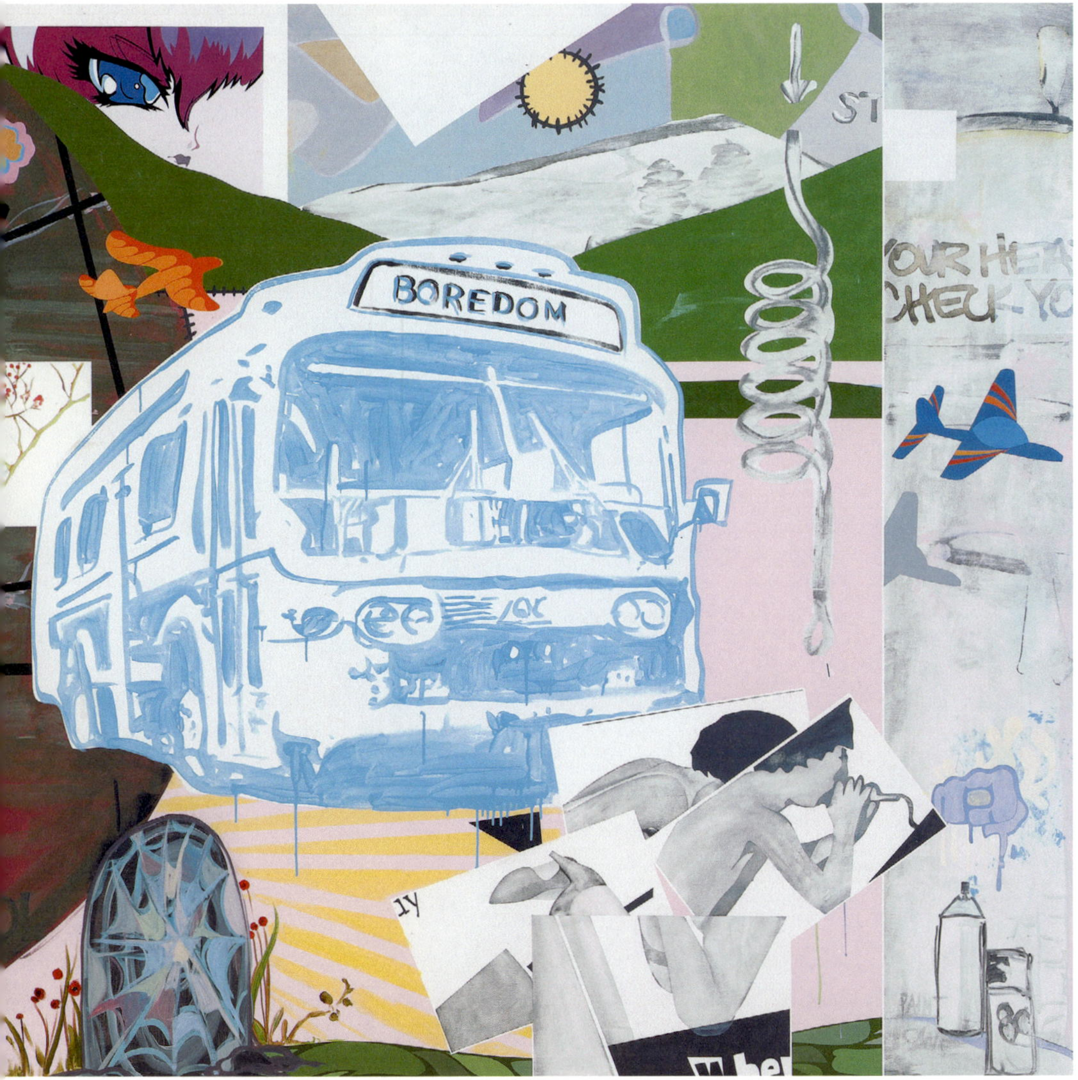
BOREDOM

New Dawn Fades. 2003

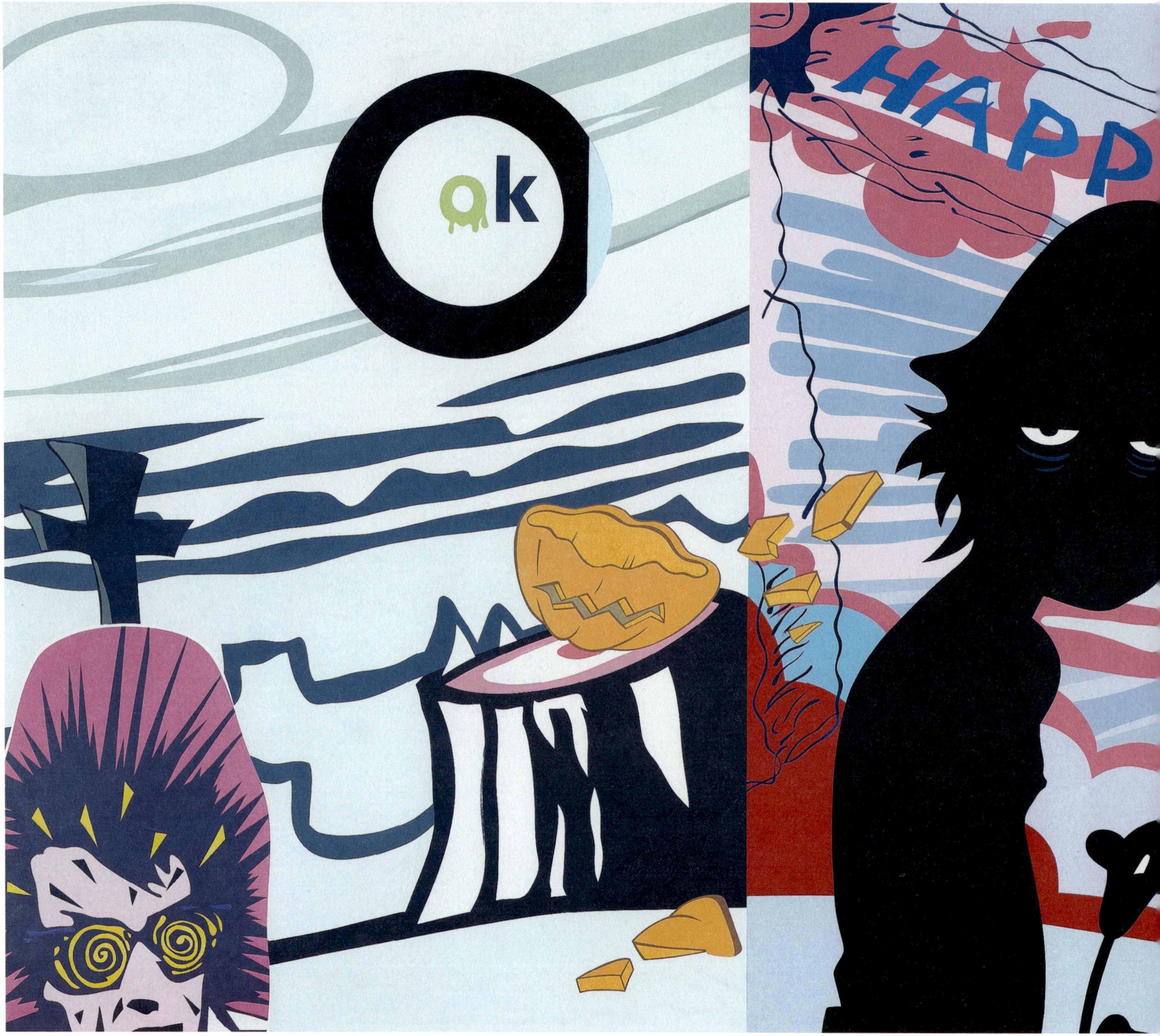

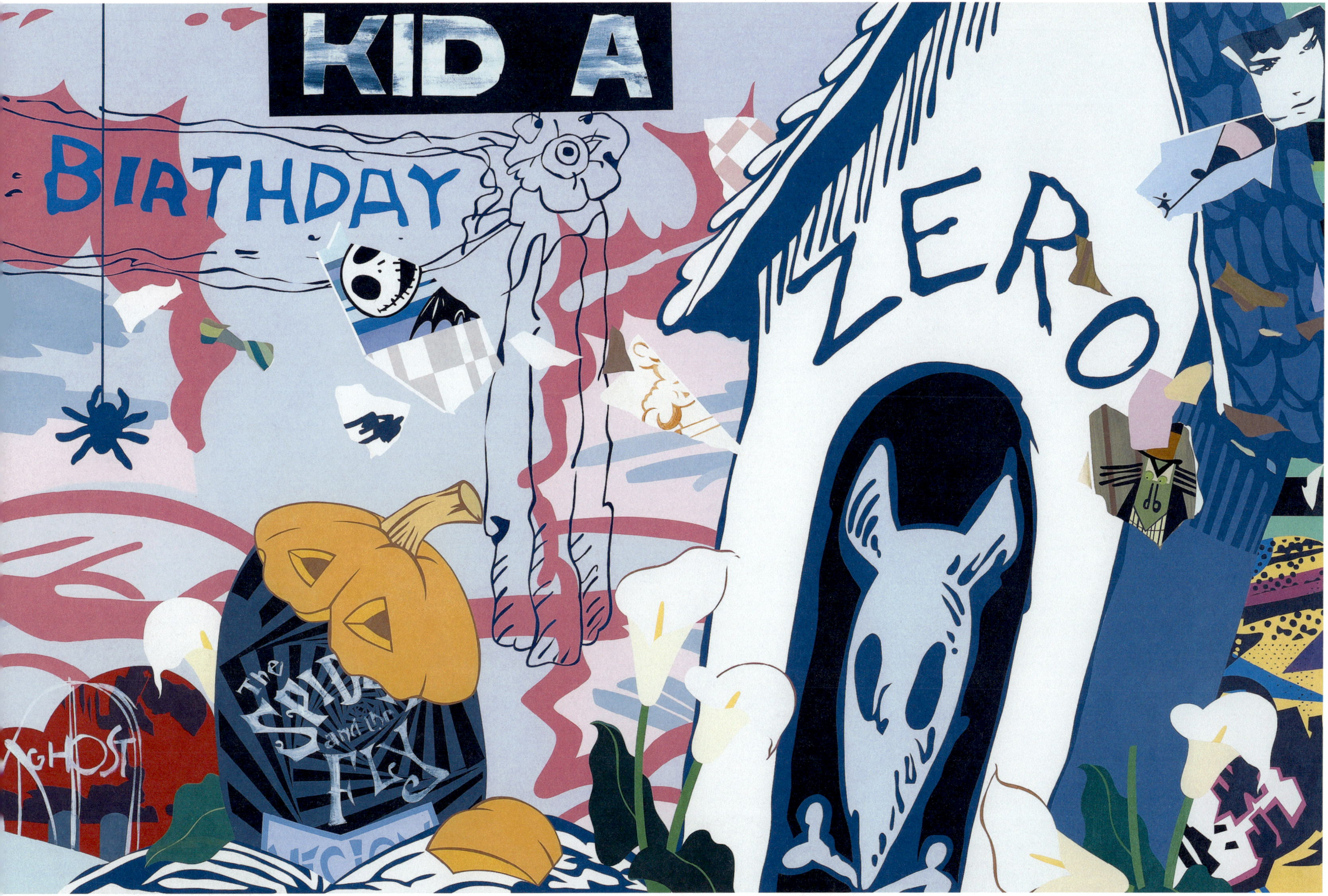
KID A
BIRTHDAY
ZERO
GHOST

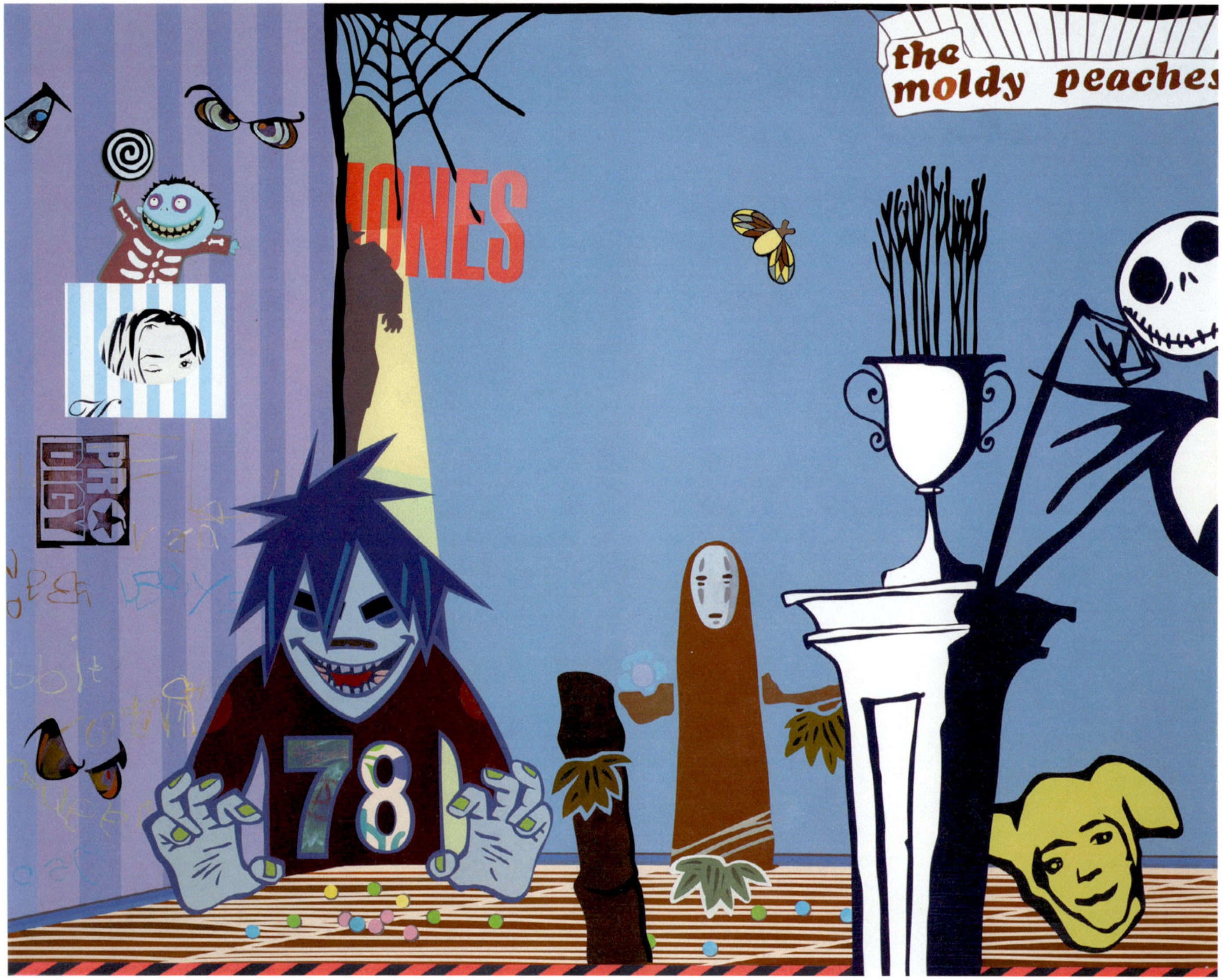
the moldy peaches
ONES
PRO
DIGY
78

Happy Nightmare Baby. 2002

SURFACE TO SPACE MICHAEL BEVILACQUA INTERVIEWED IN HIS STUDIO NYC MARCH 2005 / POUL ERIK TØJNER

PET: Just taking a brief look at your paintings reveals that music plays an important role, there are references to music all over ...

MB: Music is everything. Where I grew up in Northern California what there was was surfing and music. I remember coming home from school and instantly putting on the Ramones. In the studio I listen to music all the time while working – all kinds. I know a lot of artists work listening to talk radio, but I am not one of them. There has to be music, it has a certain energy and I usually play it really loud. Right now it's primarily old music like Bauhaus, but I listen to a lot of contemporary music as well. It distracts you in a good way, like when Picasso talked about how he did a painting and stepped back and just didn't remember doing it. Like a somnambulist. That to me is a good day in the studio, and I experienced something very similar when doing *Surface to Air*. I can see all the things that went into the painting, and I remember the music I listened to – but I don't remember actually physically painting it. It becomes a flow. To me there's no discrepancy between the two modes of sensing, sight and hearing – you can see the music and hear the painting, to put it that way. Basically it's energy. Music creates space, and painting has a lot to do with converting a surface into spatial forms, into space.

PET: So in this self-forgetting mode you are still very much present in the creative process, right?

MB: I am, and it really is a process. I never make drawn-out plans, sketches, outlines – like those diagrams that you see which are in fact more interesting than the actual resulting paintings: Maps of colorfields with little numbers in them, referring to specific colors. I could never have anybody working for me, doing parts of the canvases. Each new painting starts with just one image, the rest is totally open – I really try to be open, to let the painting tell me what is going on ... by making this first mark, the first image on the painting, I start a process, and if I have an idea about what it's going to end up with, most often when it's done, it's just totally different. It's a bit like Pollock, he just started with one drip and then ... There's no initial drawing. But I don't know if he always stuck to it and just let the painting decide, or if he was more of a canvas-shredder.

PET: You never cancel canvases yourself?

MB: No, I just go with the mistakes, I'm like a king of happy accidents. I welcome it, I think it makes painting exciting. To do a painting exactly the way it was constructed in a drawn-up plan would be immensely boring. And eventually the painting will look like that, like a … cold slice of cheese. I don't want to turn myself into a technician. I like the idea that my work has a certain human touch to it that also touches the human. In that sense the painting process in itself is my art school; it's in this process that I learn what I am about, what I am and what I really want.

PET: You described to me how you lift motifs over from various sources by scaling them up or down using the Xerox machine, then using tracing paper and tape to work layer on layer – but you do work freehand as well?

MB: I do a lot of freehand now, yes. And the thing where I brush the canvas to make it look a little dirty – it all has a drawing aspect to it. Like in the painting *Inside Looking Out;* that is of course a comment on Abstract Expressionist painting … painting that black wall and rubbing it, bringing forth images that I had no control of, then picking out the things you like and putting other things in, the freedom of that … it is in fact quite similar to the way I used to do the more graphic works … just now it's even more so, since I can do anything I want, use anything I find interesting.

PET: You are using a word now that I have grown suspicious of – the word comment. Everybody has used that word for the last twenty years, but what does it mean, comment – I mean, to you?

MB: Well, for me it isn't necessarily criticism, it can be more like giving a tip of the hat to someone, trying to get into the head of that person. But it's a little bit of everything; basically commentary, it works both ways around: I love it – and I hate it. I often take images from other painters, also contemporary painters, things that I see in galleries and that I just happen to like.

PET: Is Abstract Expressionism the worst thing that ever happened to painting?

MB: No. It sure created a lot of poor artists. But them aside, I am not against it by confession. I never really looked to Rauschenberg before, but the more I now look at this combine painting from 1955 *The Bed* ... it's incredible, an incredible mix of styles that I find highly interesting – brushstrokes, expressionist painting, ornamentation. It is fascinating that this was done so long ago, since what it really does is everything you would ascribe to the computer generation. I feel very intrigued by this freedom of styles, mixing everything up but still keeping it in the same philosophy of painting. This is a lot like what I am up to myself right now. When you've been doing the same kind of pictures for eight years, you have to in a sense throw it all away, or re-think your position. It also has to do with the passing of time in a more personal and direct way: the kids growing older, a whole new landscape of experience. You can't eliminate the diaristic element from painting – at least I can't.

PET: That's an important difference in approach compared to your 'ancestors' in Pop Art – if you take a great European Pop artist like Per Kirkeby or an American like Roy Lichtenstein, artists that technically did things similar to your work, in the sixties – they would never stress the diaristic. They would say almost the opposite: We can paint anything. But when Kirkeby looks back on his old lacquer-on-board paintings now – and when we look at Lichtenstein's – there is a sense that maybe the imagery wasn't so incidental, maybe it *was* a kind of a hidden diary. Pop was supposed to mean freedom, to be totally unbound. So it is interesting for me to hear you stress the diaristic aspect, reversing this idea ...

MB: I guess when something is absolutely new, you never know exactly what you do, you are just doing it. John Cage probably didn't think of himself as avant-garde, he was just doing his thing. In the case of Kirkeby, he may now realize that he *did* have a certain connection to this horse and the mountains that he took from Tin Tin. And I've heard that Warhol did in fact for a long period have tomato soup for lunch every day. But in a way I envy them this innocence, this initial sense of freedom.

PET: Your paintings have these two very closely-connected features or modes, each of which nevertheless works in its own way with the recipient – the recognizable figures and the color. Can you say anything about your relation to color; do you think in color?

MB: In the more graphic paintings the elements are like features, they create color fields and gaps. Color now is becoming real points of interest. It has changed a lot for me; the colors have changed a lot. They were extremely bright paintings, the graphic works, while the new ones are subdued. Watching a movie with my kids three years ago, *Tim Burton's Nightmare Before Christmas*, with almost exclusively black, green, brown tones, I realized that I was myself on the verge of entering another or broader spectrum of color that fits better with the multitude of experiences and emotions that I need to comprehend.

PET: Some of the paintings I see as a kind of statement that even in the figurative, there is abstraction – though they are figurative, you can see them as abstract paintings ...

MB: I think you're right.

PET: When thinking in terms of Art History, we used to have the preoccupation that the experience of the artist is not just the experience of this individual, but in a sense the experience of a generation or in a broader sense the experience of humanity at a certain point. But is this also true of the modern or post-modern artist like yourself? Are we being confronted with the Bevilacqua story in front of your pictures, or are we still to some degree partaking in the same general story of human experience? Can you still tell the Story of Our Time, or is your artistic universe much more private?

MB: I don't think it's private at all. What I do is I tie up elements from everyday life with very iconic images from various transitional stages of my life. Everybody has an everyday life, and everybody's going through transitional phases. I enjoy the responses from other people, and in fact one of my reasons for putting all these images in the pictures is that people relate to them. It brings a social aspect into the work. Right now I'm diving into an imagery that belongs to a period in my life that goes back some fifteen years. So of course there is a personal layer, but I don't think you need a key to the meaning. The feeling is the meaning. My work has even become more personal in this sense, as the canvases now hold more drama. The more graphic works were cooler, but life itself becomes more of a drama. There is simultaneously an openness that comes with having so much more complexity in your actual life, and on the other hand an artistic introspection, spending so much time alone in the studio. But it all makes sense in the end. And it isn't private. It's painting.

PET: How do you know that you are an artist?

MB: It's very funny that you ask, because whenever at parties people ask me what I do, I answer that I'm a painter. "You mean you paint houses and stuff?" – and I go "Yeah." So my wife asks me, why don't you tell them that you're an artist? But I don't know what that is, to be an artist. I'm a painter.

Poul Erik Tøjner (b. 1959) has a PhD in Literature with a dissertation on Søren Kierkegaard. He is since 2000 the director of Louisiana Museum of Modern Art, Denmark.

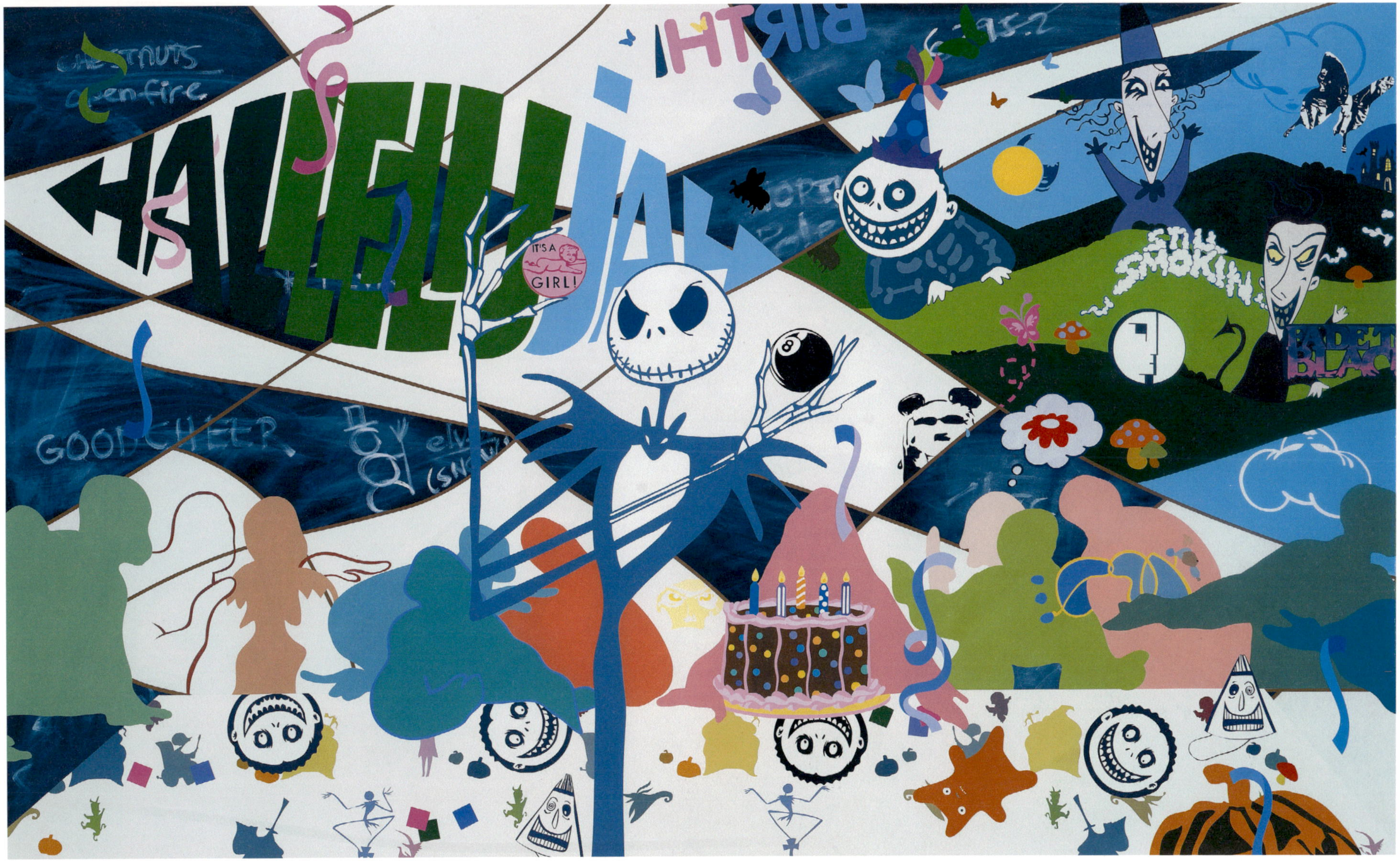
IT'S A GIRL!

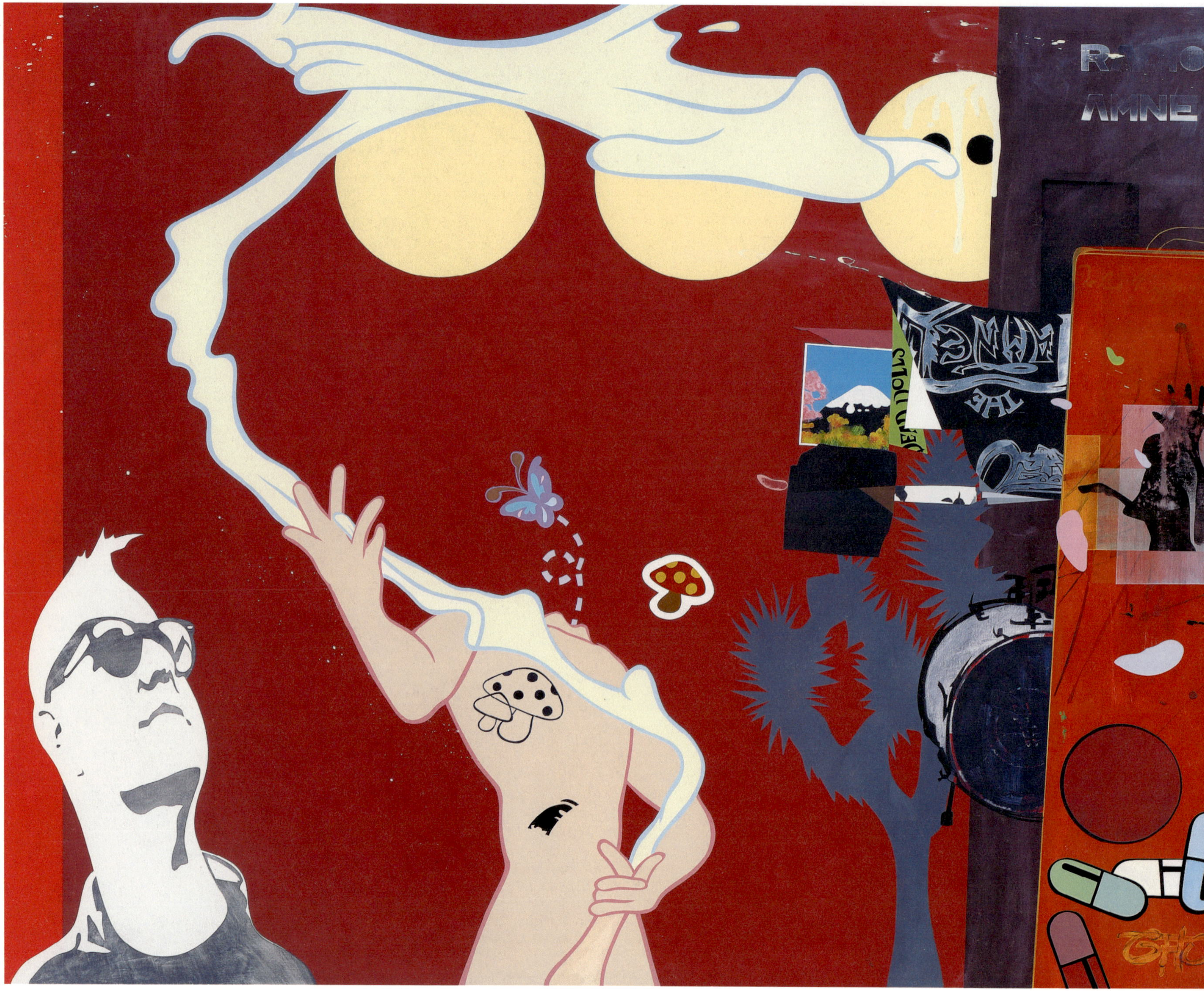

Decline of Western Civilization. 2003

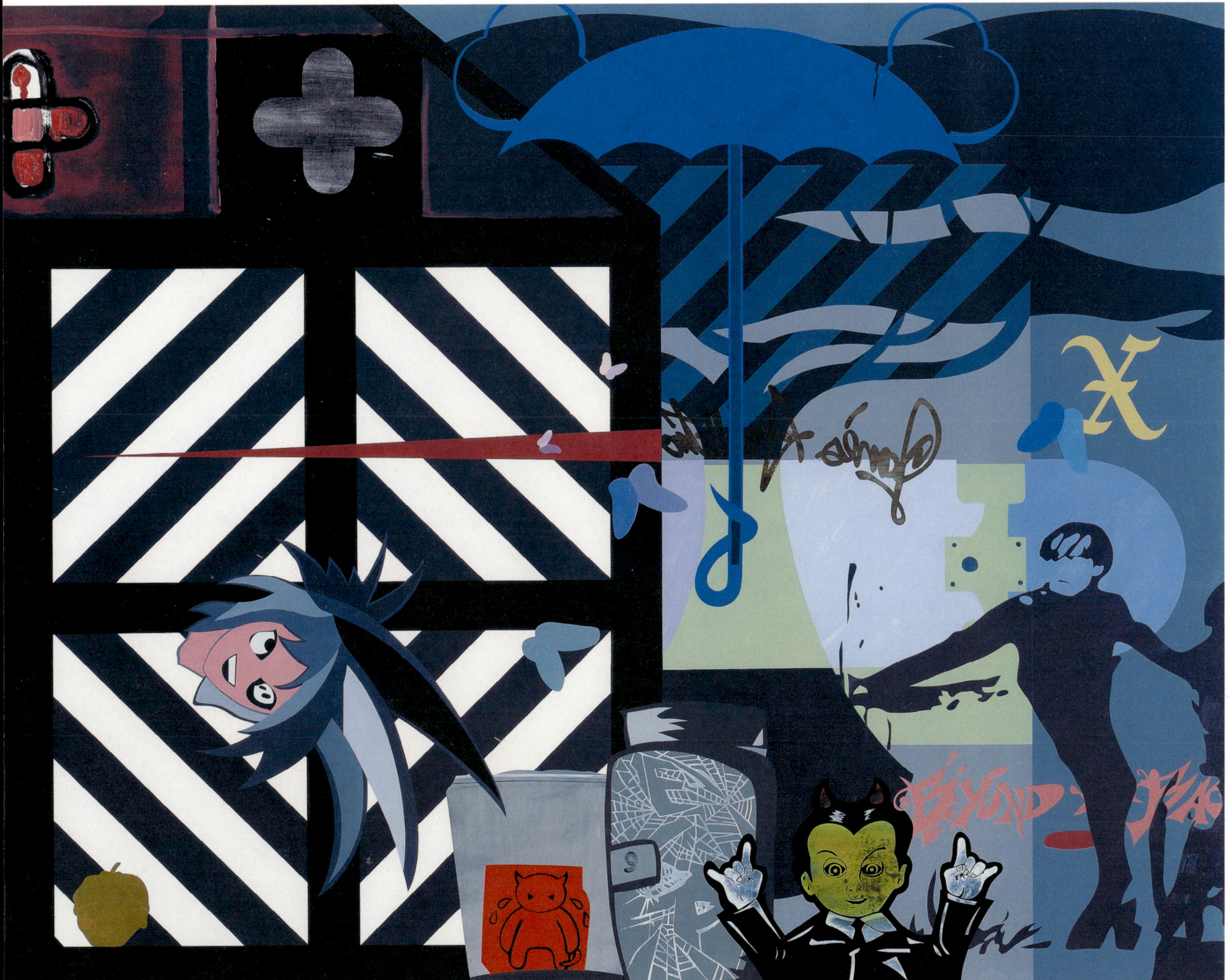

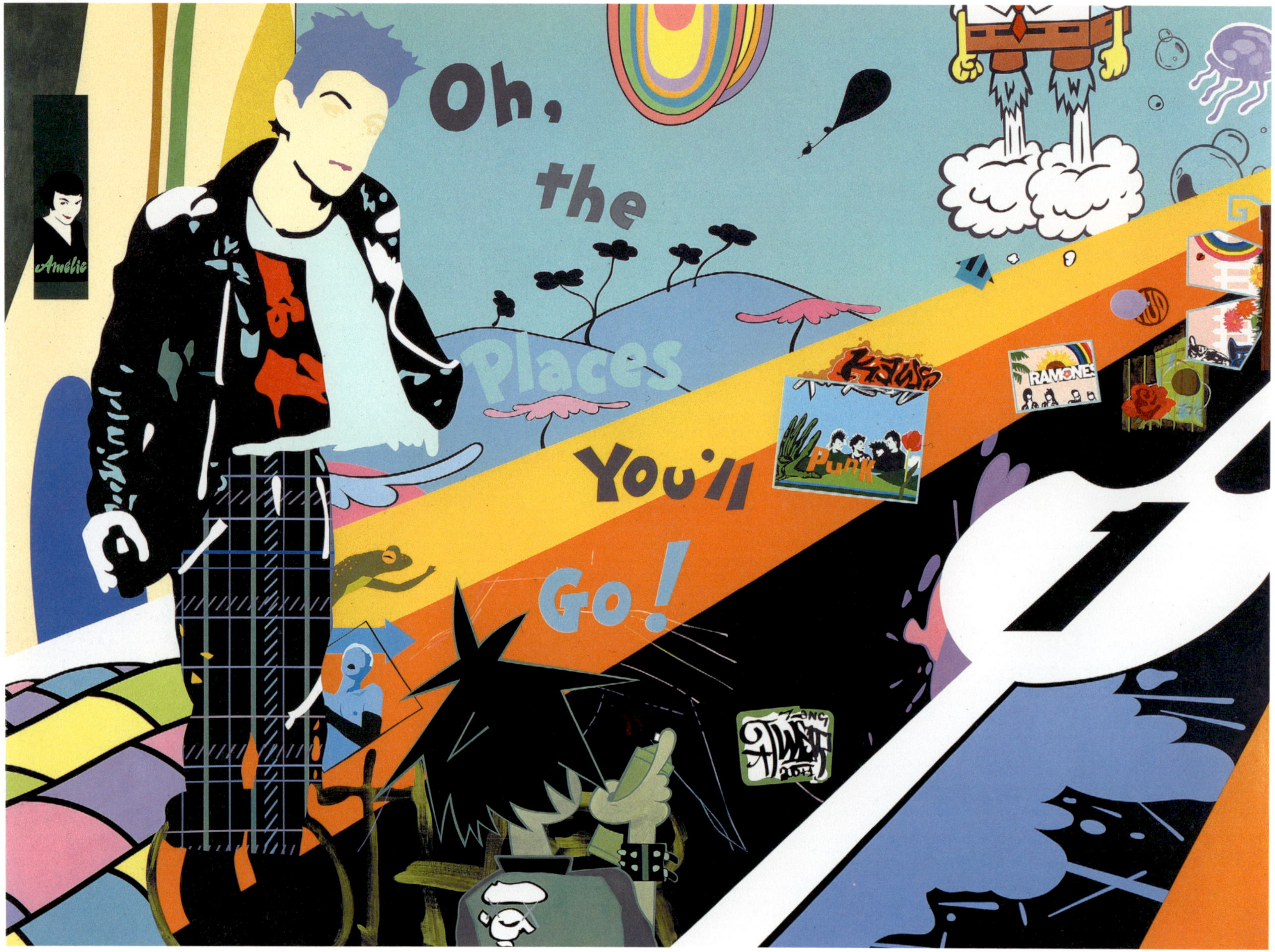

Zero. 2002

M1 - A1 (Teenage Wasteland). 2002

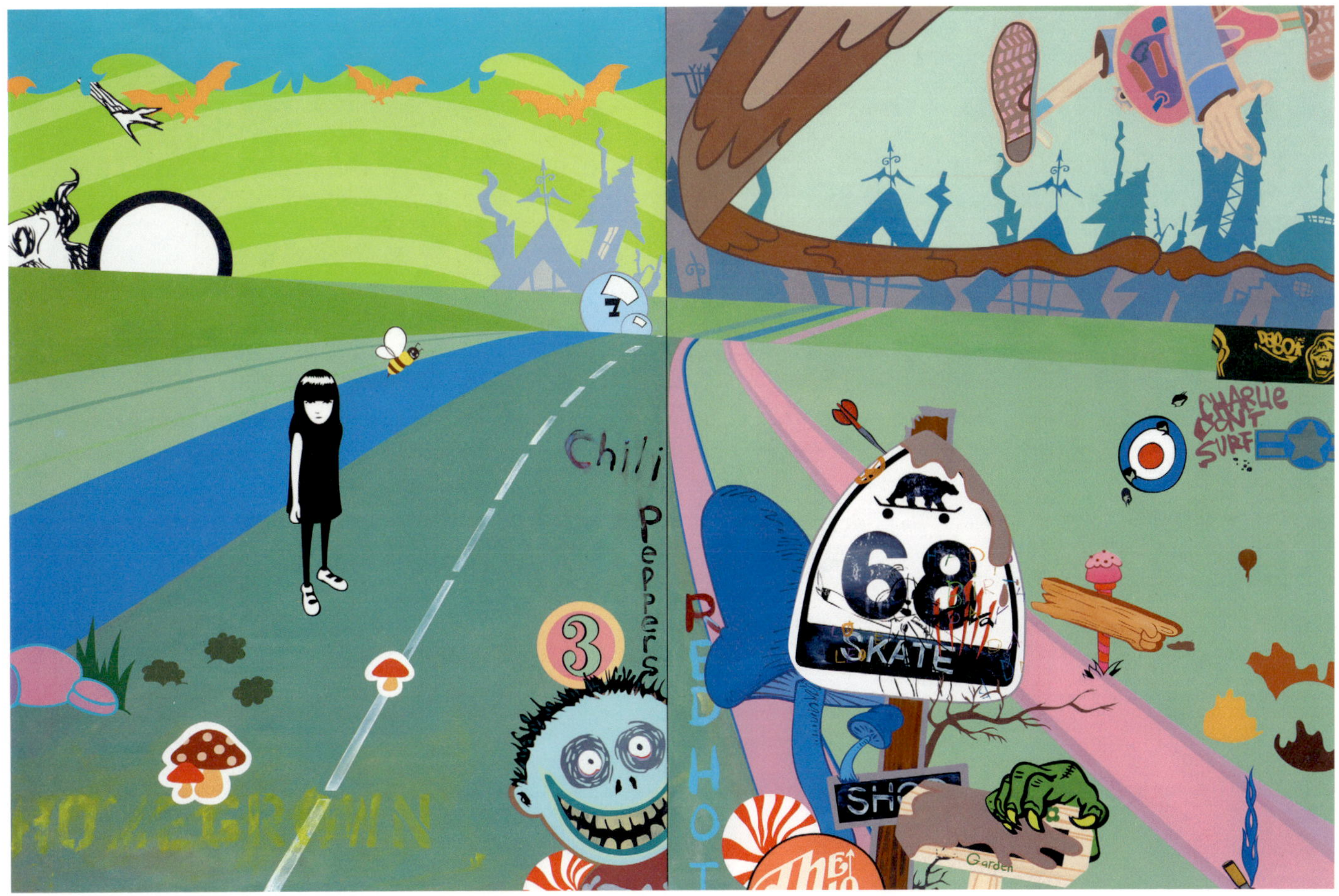

Gabba Gabba Hey. 2002

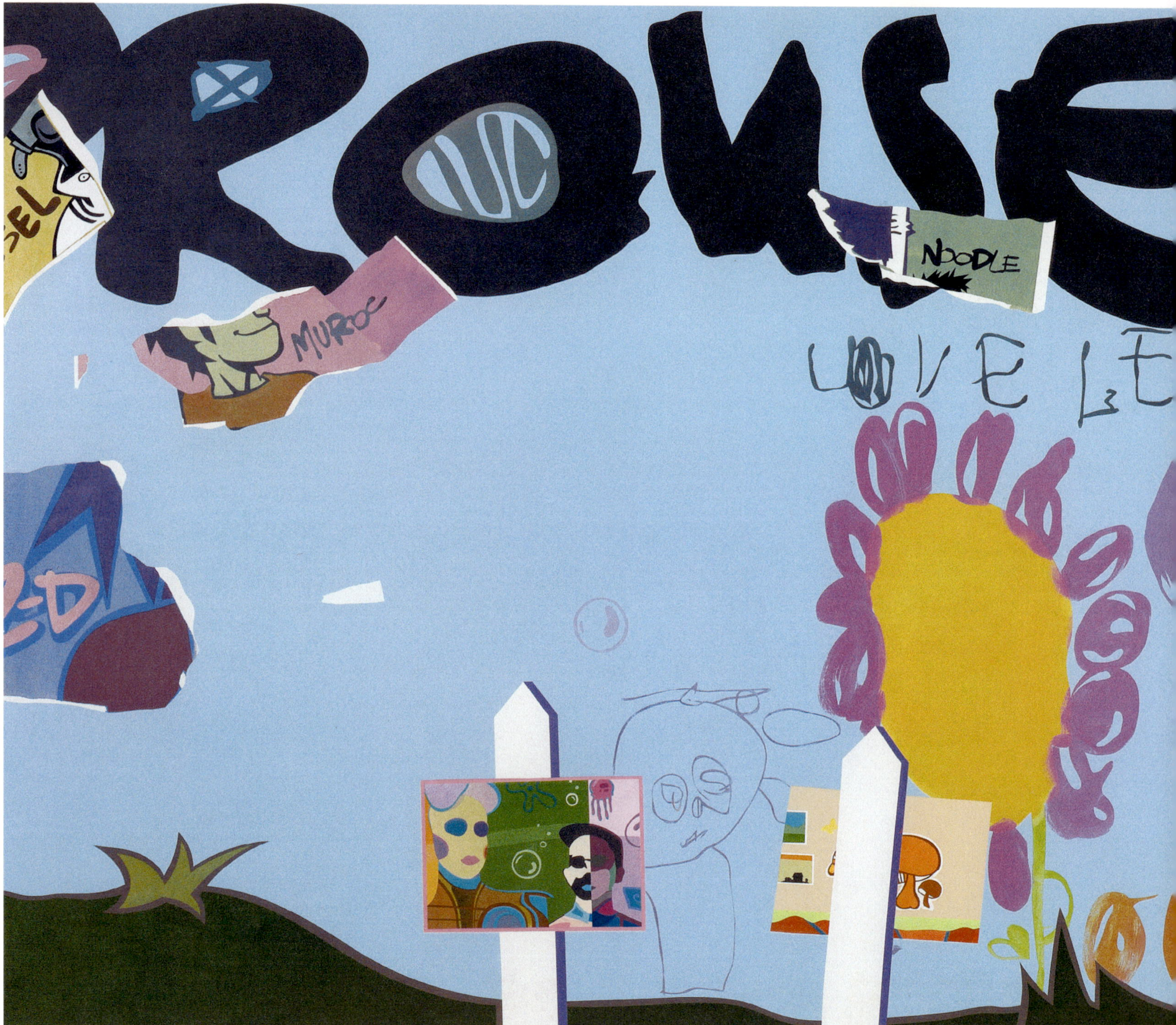

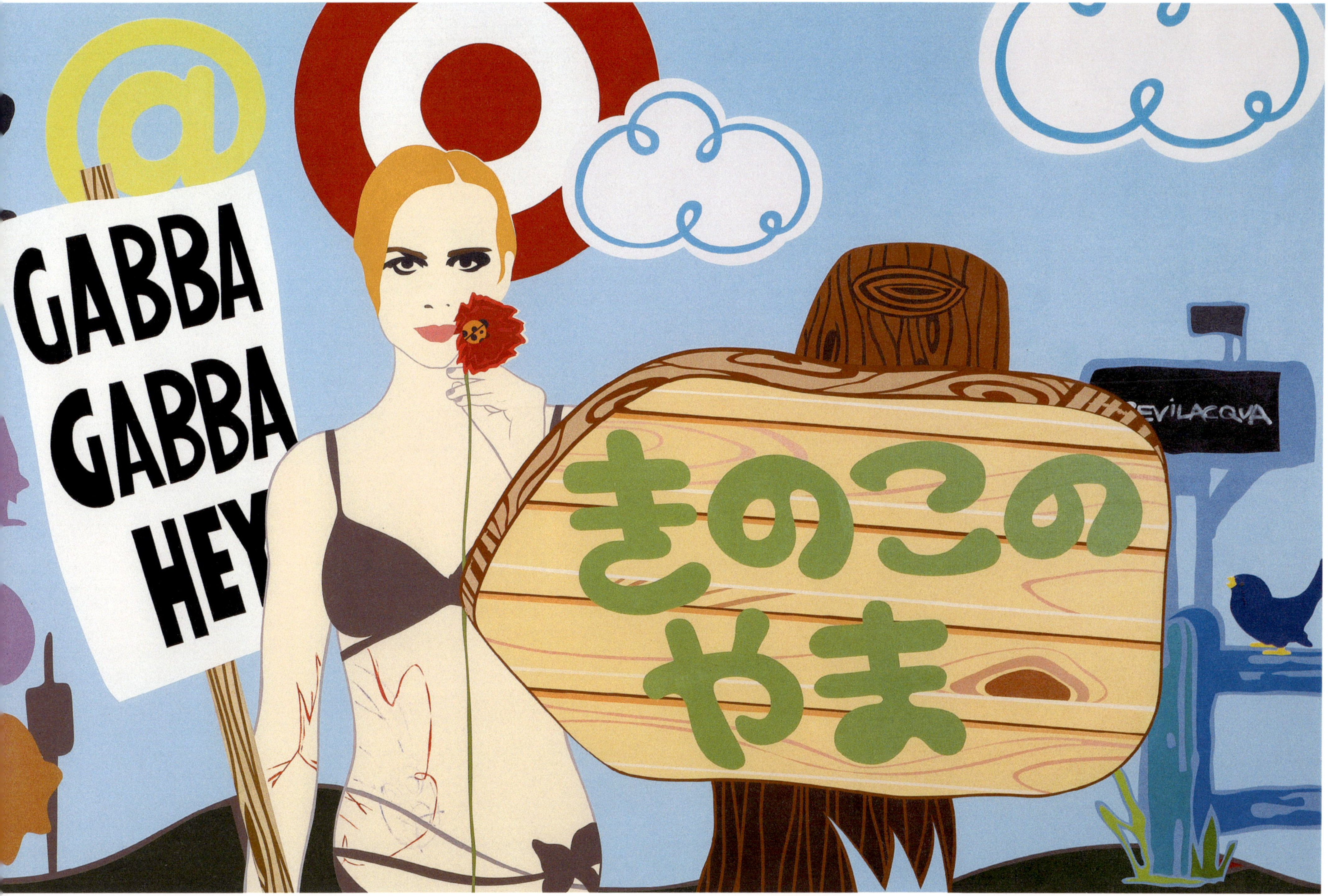
GABBA
GABBA
HEY
きのこの
やま
BEVILACQUA

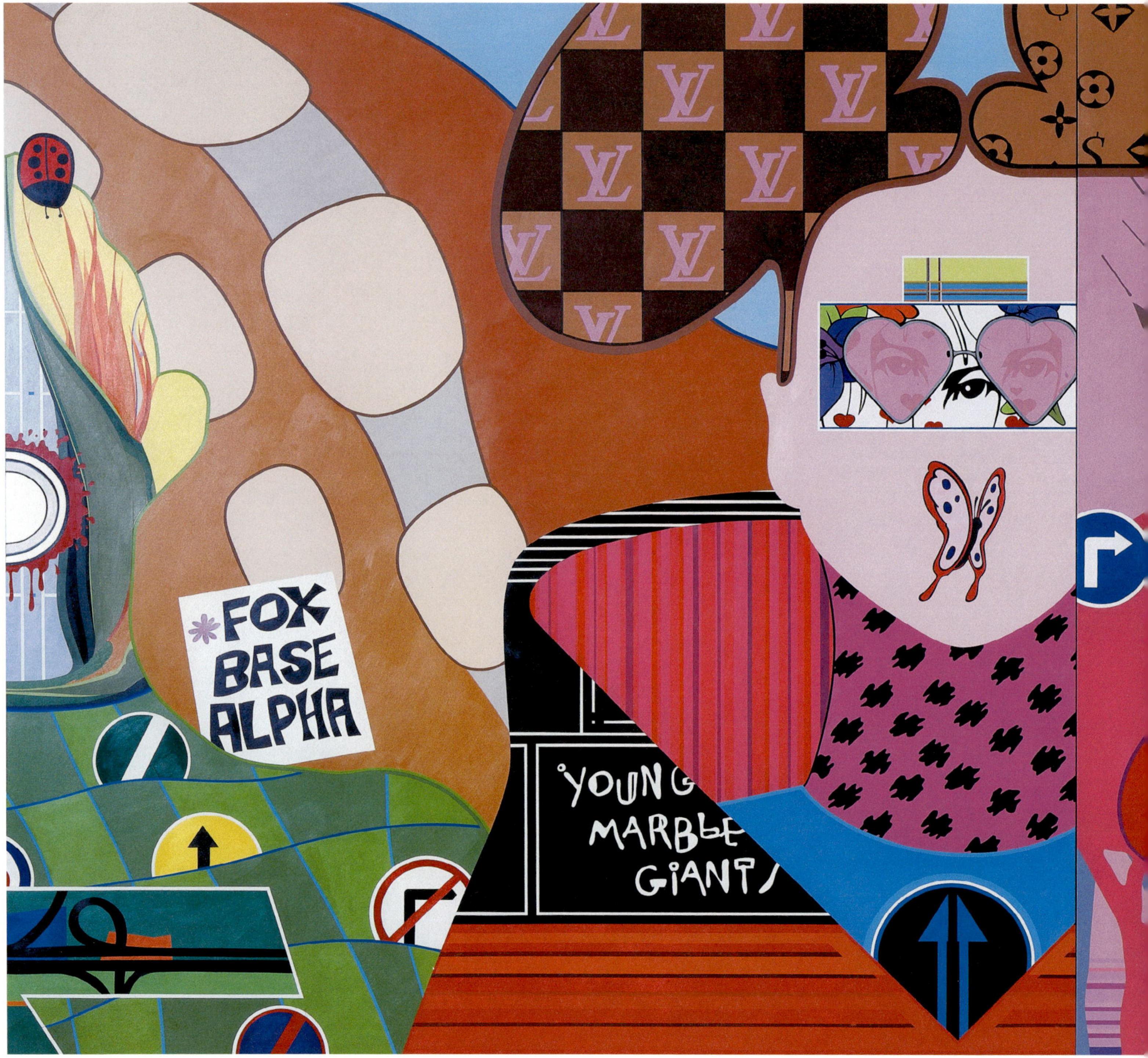

Picnic by the Motorway. 2000

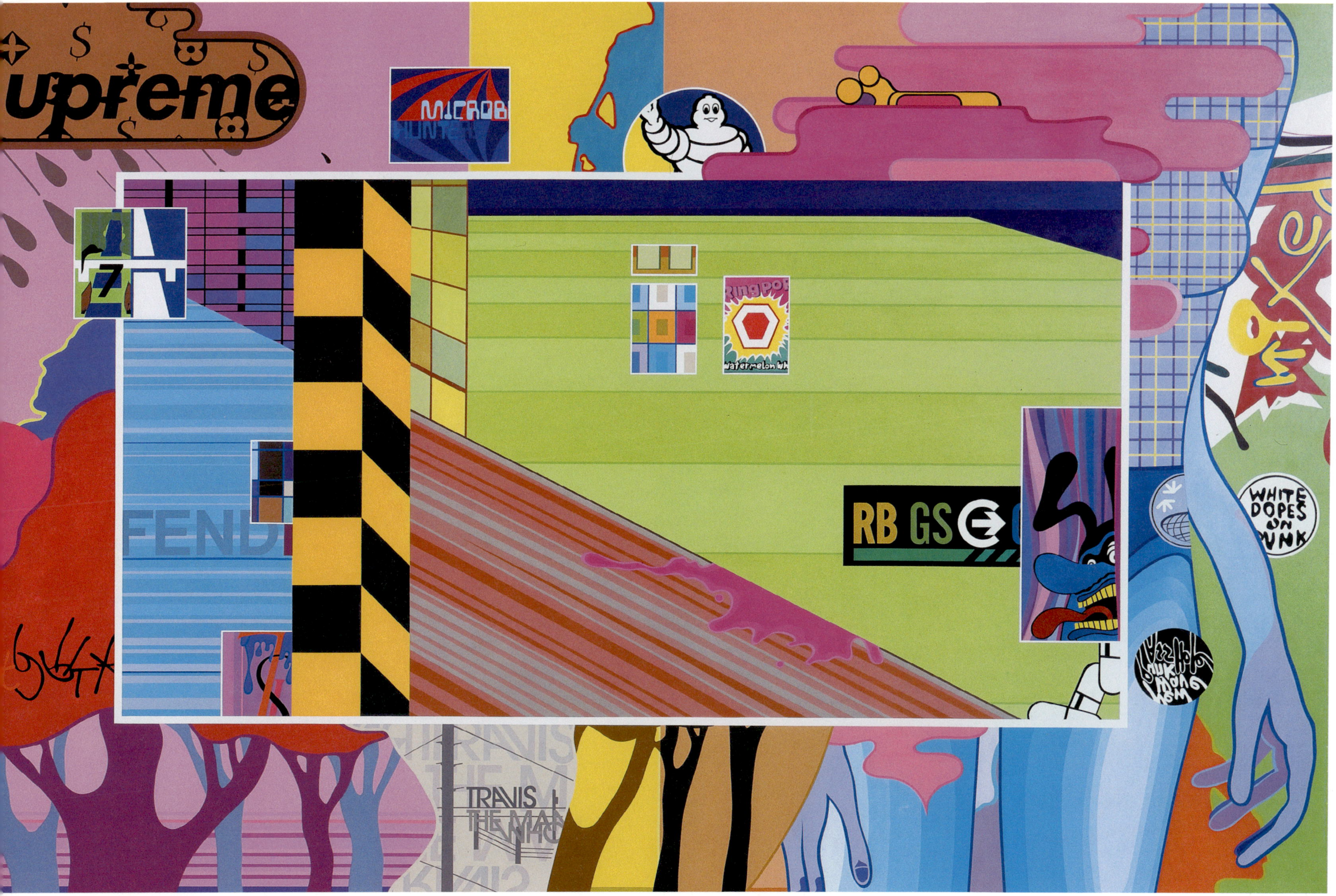
upreme
MICROB
FEND
RB GS
TRAVIS
THE MA
WHITE DOPES ON UNK

Leave Home. 2001

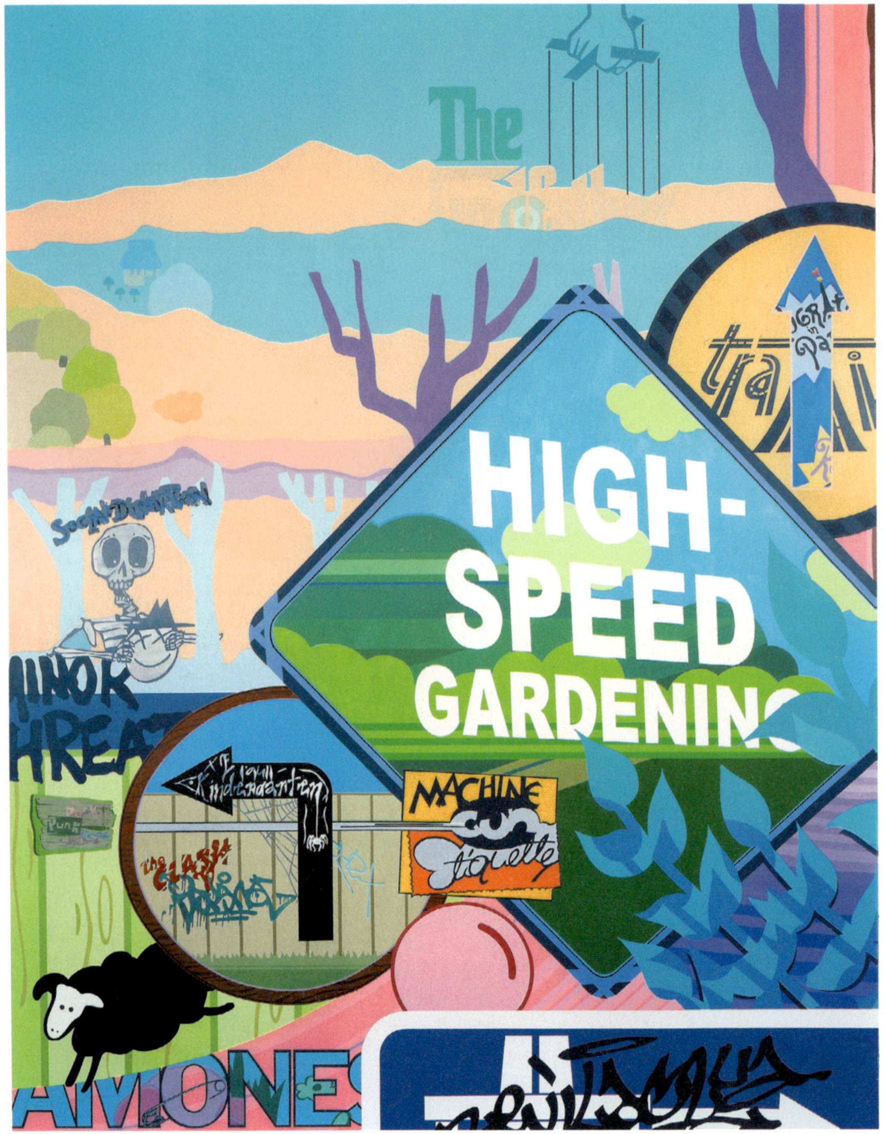

High-Speed Gardening. 2000 >

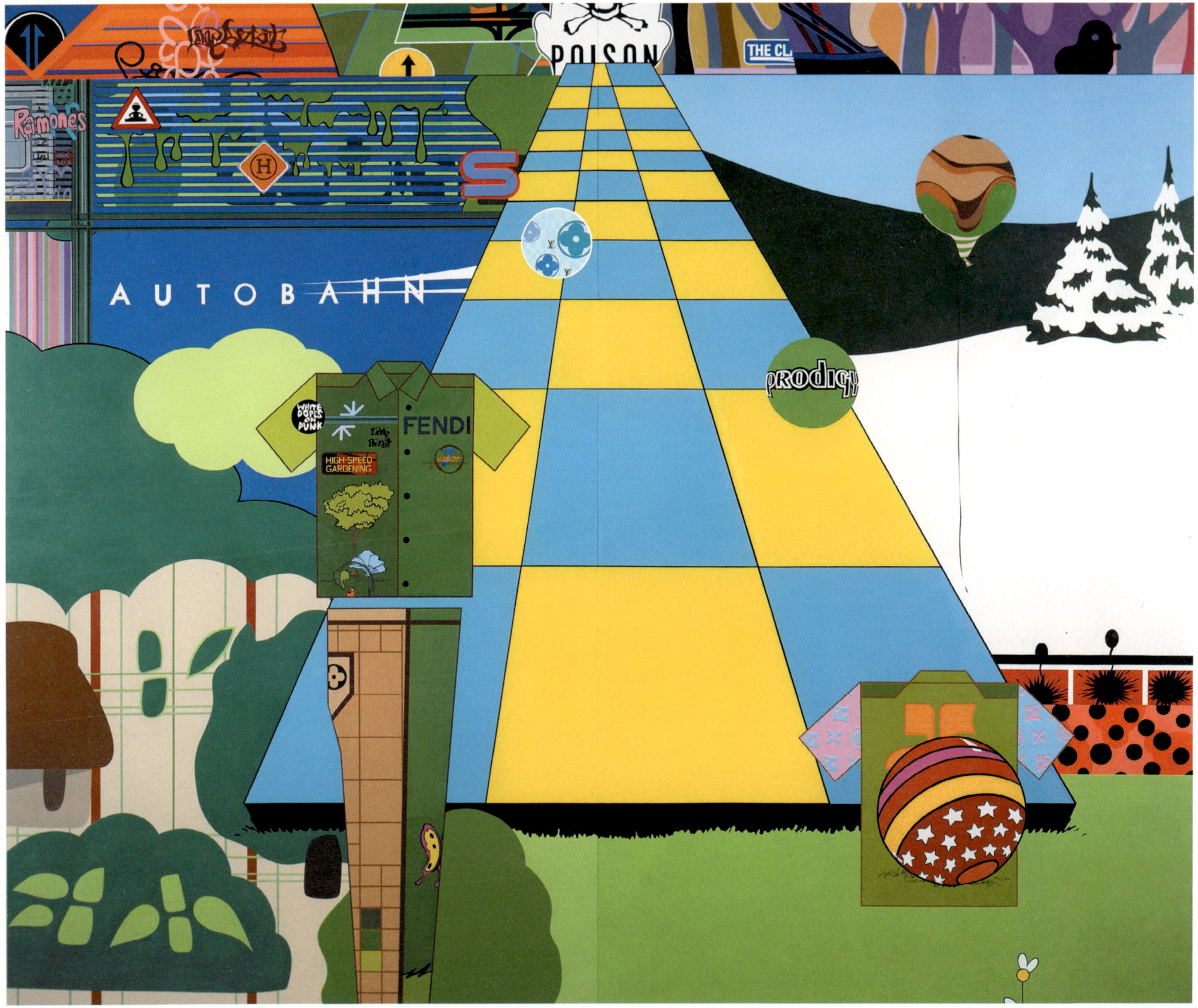
POISON
Ramones
AUTOBAHN
FENDI
WHITE DOPES ON PUNK
HIGH-SPEED GARDENING
prodigy

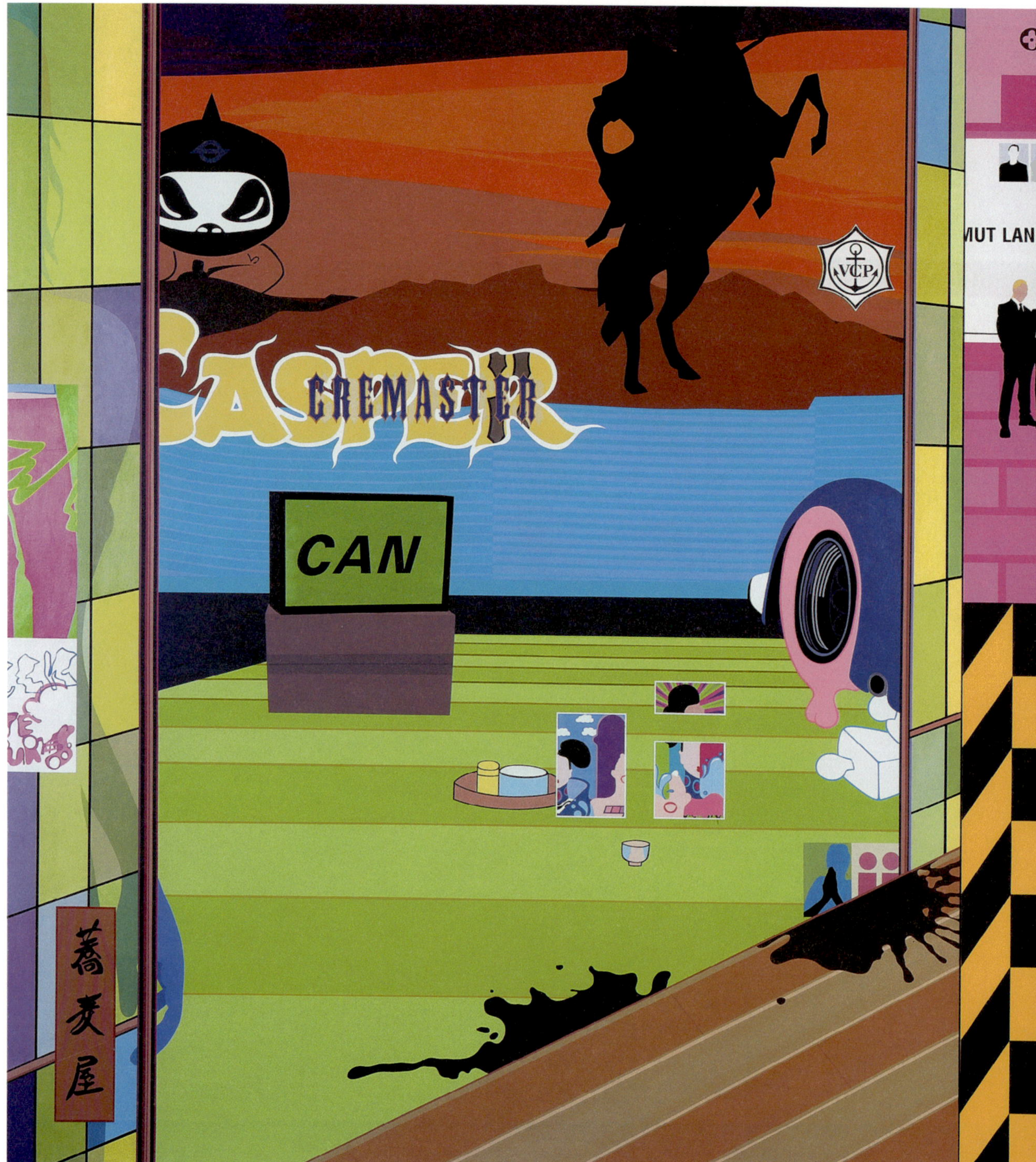

Shut Up, I'm Meditatin'. 1999

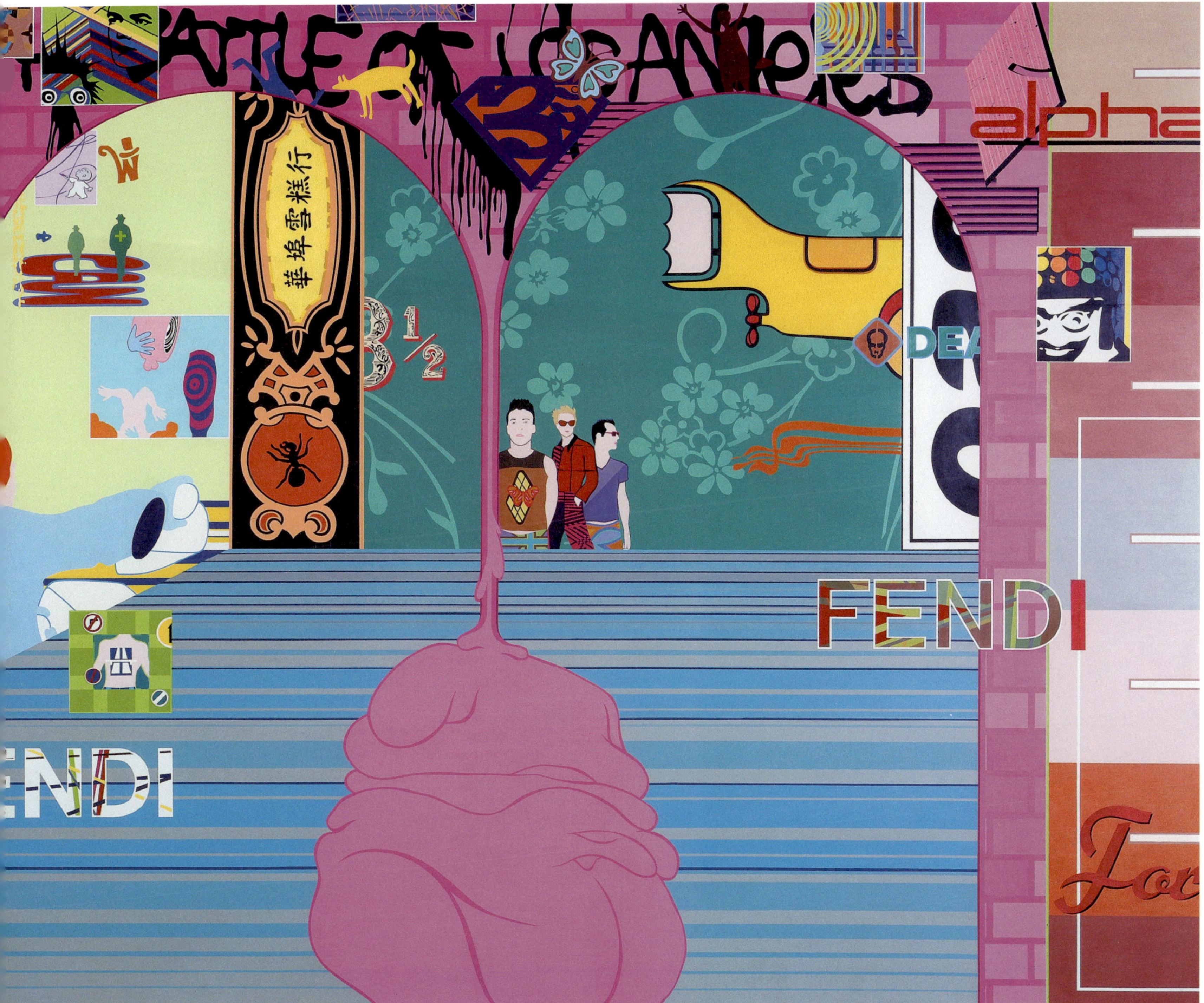
alpha
華埠雪糕行
FENDI
ENDI
DEA

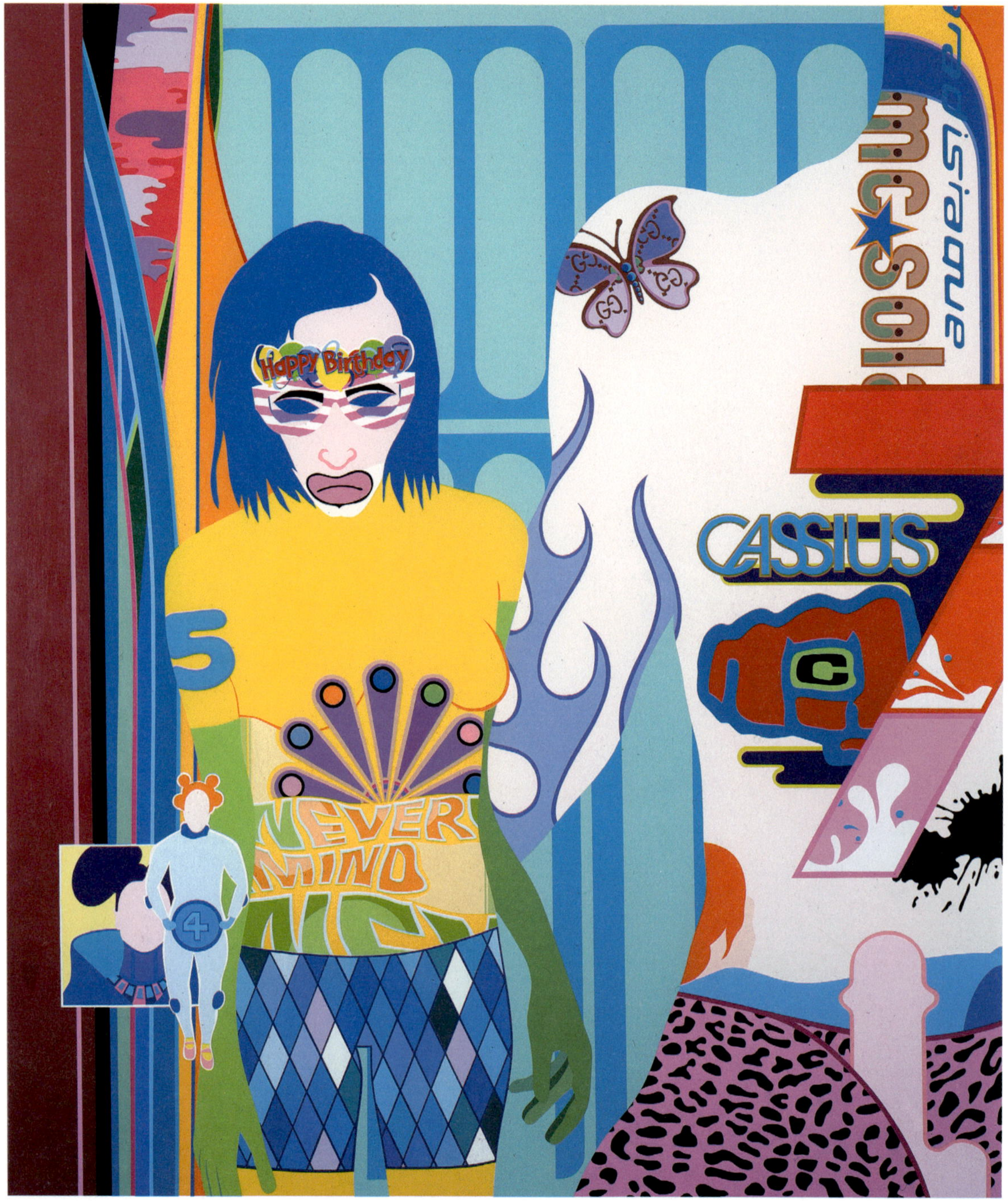

Teen Spirit, 1999

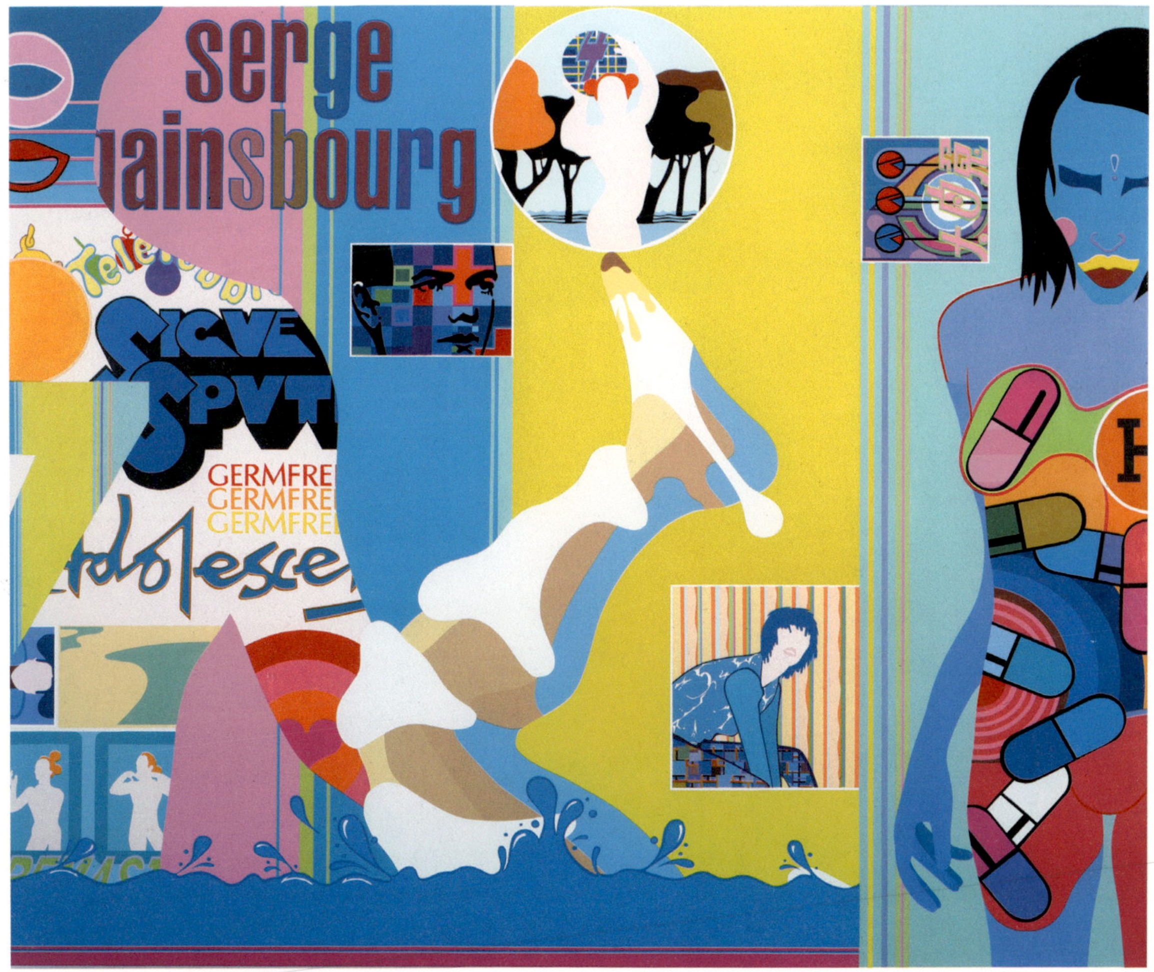

Atom Tan. 1999

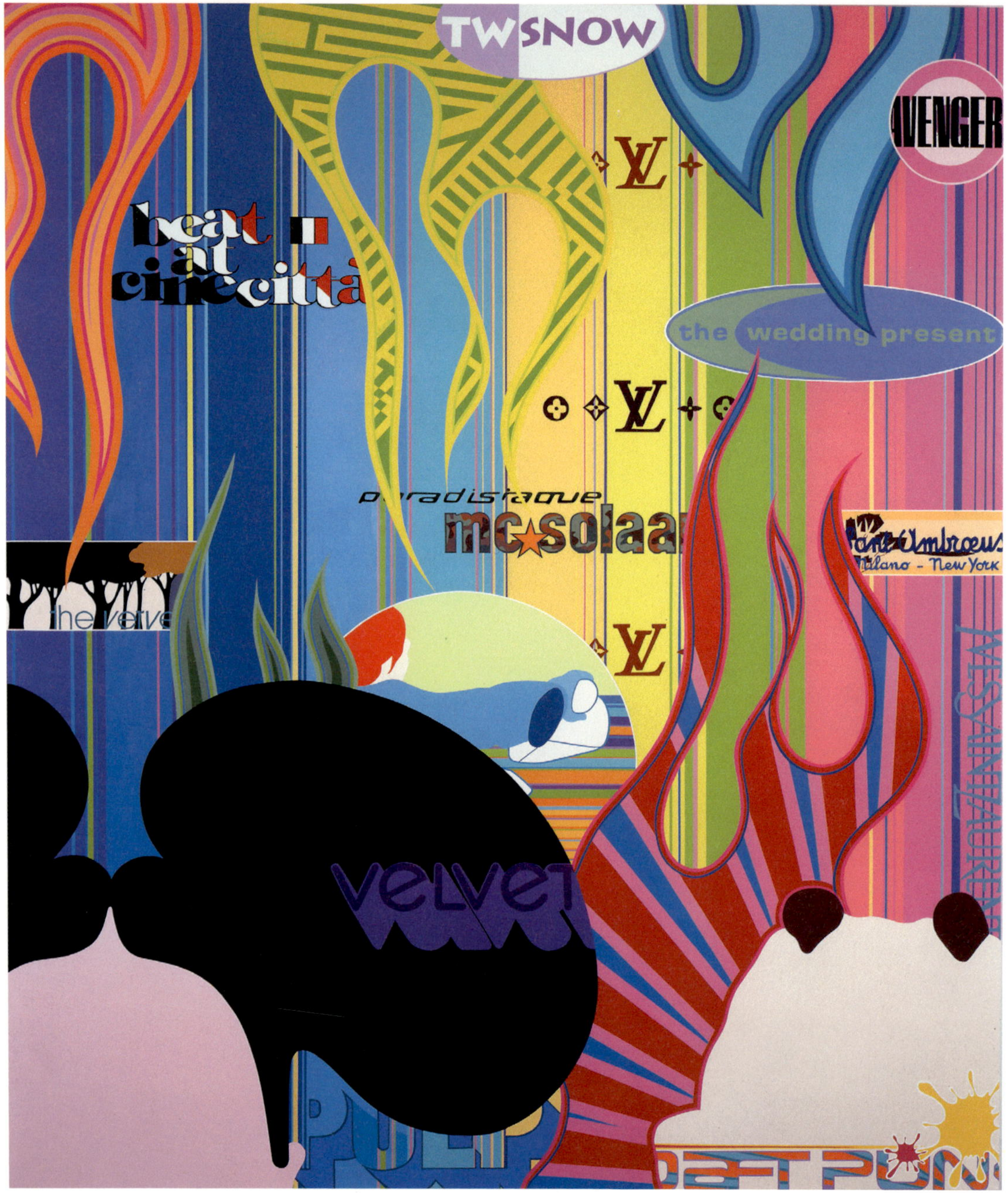
TWSNOW
AVENGER
beat at cinecittà
the wedding present
paradistaque
mc solaar
Milano - New York
velvet
PULP

FESTINA LENTE — QUICK BUT SLOW / MICHAEL JUUL HOLM

If you wanted to pin labels on the American painter Michael Bevilacqua's work so far – so far, because the man, in spite of everything, is not yet forty – it would have to be something to do with sampling, postmodernity and the zap culture. In that sense there's something seductively self-evident about his art for a whole generation – my own – that grew up in the sixties and the seventies and was young in the eighties and nineties. A generation of so-called symbol analysts who (so they say, but then again...) can negotiate a universe of logos, trademarks, culture industry symbols and insider allusions to all sorts of pop and underground phenomena as naturally as the old-time peasant with his weather eye and the indigenous Polynesian navigators who took their bearings from the water temperature, the length of the waves and the positions of the stars in the sky.

Bevilacqua's earliest canvases in particular pile up a wealth of both familiar and more apocryphal figures from the late modern firmament of backlit and high-gloss visual signs. In his iconic kaleidoscope you can find logos for fashion houses like Fendi, Louis Vuitton and Yves Saint Laurent and recognizable graphic symbols from record covers – from the Beatles' *Yellow Submarine* and the Velvet Underground to German 'Kraut rock' groups and French rap; as well as a veritable Hall of Fame of figures from the pop culture of the past thirty years.

Here we find those with the mental late-night passes like the punk icons The Ramones, the eighties Gothic Grue pastiche group The Cramps, *Tim Burton's The Nightmare Before Christmas*, and elements from the video artist Matthew Barney's *Cremaster Cycle* – as well as the more innocuous items: the cute and cuddly *Care Bears*, Paramount Pictures' classic cartoon figure *Casper the Friendly Ghost* (60 years old today!) and Andy Warhol's stylized garish flowers (or on closer inspection – is it Elizabeth Arden's sunflower symbol?). The comfort animals of the MTV generation come from all cultural strata and populate all the nooks and crannies of consciousness. It's almost like a visual attack on the philosophical godfather of the eighties, Baudrillard. Meanings that go into orbit, simulacra-shmimulacra – and the same to you! Presenting the postmodernism to end all postmodernisms.

The time of painting

All the same that isn't the right thing to do – I mean pin a quick label on him. At least it isn't the only thing to do. For you won't find any speed-painting in Bevilacqua's pictures. True, his earliest penchant as a visual artist, by his own account, was for racing cars, more specifically the rich, composite pictorial world you meet in the American motor-sports mixture of pure décor and sponsors' logos in the Champ Car and Indy Car series, America's answer to the European Formula One races. And the cars still hold a special place in the artist's heart. A full-scale model decorated with all the trimmings is in the exhibition at Louisiana – a Bevilacquamobile.

But the paintings are laboriously, almost pedantically constructed with a technique that recalls the young Per Kirkeby from the sixties (Danish painter; if you don't know him, look him up, he's really interesting!), where figures from (media) reality are contoured up, carefully masked off and inserted as picture elements on the canvas, layer on layer, so that the contours and the individual colours stand out razor-sharp. No action painting or graffiti here. Yet it isn't only this toilsome working process, the back-to-front archaeology or what you could call the geology of the painting that slows down the flow of meaning in the pictures. It's first and foremost the way you have to step with caution as a spectator – of all painting, and not least when it comes to a serious joker like Michael Bevilacqua, who deliberately plays on the distance between the ad-hoc fellowship and instant accessibility of pop culture and the slow-motion, delayed-action effects of the actual medium – painting.

For what is true to some extent of photography, drawings and various graphic idioms is even more intensely true of painting. The saying goes that a picture 'is worth a thousand words', and you immediately feel that even that is something of an understatement. In reality a good painting says something that can't be said with any amount of words. I'll spare the reader the more egg-headed pronouncements about the special phenomenological status and temporality of painting, but there are some obvious and important points to be grasped by simply standing in front of a painting and taking a proper look; even just by virtue of the materiality and texture, the canvas, the frame, the brushstrokes ... and in Bevilacqua's case something as simple and conspicuous (and therefore often overlooked) as its size – after all, we live in the age of reproduction and digitalization, when everything is equally big, in the book and on the screen. In other words, by virtue of its physicality alone the painting demands the attention of the viewer over a period of time: it can't be sensed in a glimpse.

And the content-components of the painting – whether we're looking at true realism, still life, collage or something that approaches pure abstraction – are *always* taken from many different places and therefore refer to themselves, or more precisely to the work they are becoming part of, rather than to 'reality'. Painting as practice – and Michael Bevilacqua is first and foremost a painter – is an art form that covers up and excludes something (from the world) in order to let something else appear – that is, the picture. To scan all these manoeuvres and get some idea of what we are looking at – not necessarily in a thousand words, perhaps rather as a wordless complex of sensations – we have to get both close up and far away. And that takes time.

Colour composition and memory images

So what kind of painting is it that Bevilacqua does? First, we can take the obvious fact that the man is a classic colorist, a fearless adherent to rule number one in painting: colours create space. Whereas the draughtsman has to work with perspective as lines and vanishing-points, the painter can use the juxtaposition of just two colours to create a space that negates the two-dimensionality of the surface. If I call Bevilacqua fearless it is because his talent and skill extend to the use of the whole palette: like a Matisse he plunges with the greatest natural aplomb into a controlled orgy of colours that is normally the domain of far older artists, people with the arrogance of age who permit themselves plenary indulgence in colour.

If you screw up your eyes a bit so that all the many signs and figures in the pictures fade out, what remains is first and foremost colour compositions in perfect balance. Some of the early pictures like *Do you remember the first time?* from 1998 or *Teen Spirit* from 1999 in fact have similarities to the Op-Art of the sixties; demonstrations of painterly potential with simple patterns and strong colours, a perpetuation of the tradition of *defying* the tradition, that is the ground rules for what you can and must do as a painter: if you can, you must, all the way. Here you can almost hear the youthfully virile painter's (in fact quite characteristic and oft-erupting) laughter from the canvas: "Look, I'm using purple! I'm using pink! Ha-ha! And loud green right beside it!" And it all works, it's demonstratively good.

If I mention Matisse, though, it isn't just to try to suggest the emancipated, devil-may-care coloristic talent. It's also to lend some historical weight to my objection to quick labelling, to my point that Bevilacqua's compilatory technique – the way he creates imaginary spaces by filling the picture space with all sorts of things that strictly speaking have nothing to do with one another (except, that is, that they obviously all play a part in the painter's personal universe) – isn't necessarily something generation-specific.

If it's sampling to borrow figures and patterns from vastly different spheres of reality and to use them to create an entirely new space, then Matisse was a sampler with the best of them. If it's zapping when you have to focus alternately on this and that, on the pattern of the wallpaper and the metal frame of the bedstead, the apples on the table and the window that opens, not on the world but on the picture's own geometry, then Matisse was a zapper – zap, zap! And he probably was – a zapper with scissor-hands (if the remote control had been invented by then, his sick bed and thus the history of art might have looked quite different!).

But it's nothing new or alien to the history of art; you can draw a long line from Matisse through a Pop Artist like Robert Rauschenberg, whose pictures from the sixties didn't leave Bevilacqua unaffected, to the elective affinities of the generation immediately before his own – people like Ashley Bickerton, who painted 'self-portraits' in the eighties built up solely from logos; like Lari Pittman, who in a much denser and more Surrealist-inspired style still lies close to Bevilacqua; or like the Japanese Takashi Murakami, from whom Bevilacqua has borrowed a couple of figures. (Another Murakami comes to mind – the writer Haruki Murakami, with whom Bevilacqua shares his both emphatic and empathetic approach to the modern symbols of pleasure, style and entertainment). Or a peer like the late German Michel Majerus. And to take a step further back in history – and further into an understanding of what Bevilacqua is up to, I think – the Dutch still life and the whole subsequent related history of art is there for the taking.

Cool medium

Bevilacqua's works can be seen as painted notice boards, as coloristic cousins of the modern middle-class home's silent collective repository of message, memory, proclamation, decoration and shopping list – in other words the fridge door, which with its selection of magnets shaped like multicoloured fruits, animals, buttons and all kinds of kitsch keeps track of a multitude of things that belong together there and nowhere else (sometimes you think the fridge door is currently so well composed that you agonize over adding anything or taking anything away. But then fortunately there are children – they don't have this nostalgia for the frozen moment).

On my own first encounter with Michael Bevilacqua's painting a linguistic trace from the past instantly popped into my mind – a title I had memorized when I was eleven and which (along with words like 'neuro-psychoendocrinology') I've been holding in readiness ever since. It was the title of a Danish volume combining two Tom Wolfe collections and can be translated ***The Kandy-Kolored Tangerine-Flake Streamline Baby Meets The Pump House Gang***. The Pump House Gang I was looking at was The Ramones, and the picture that triggered off the memory was ***Busy, Busy, Sunny Day***, which hung on an end wall and simply reeked of both style and still life. The museum quickly decided to buy the painting, which is now one of those you can be sure people will look long at and question the perplexed museum staff about whenever exhibited.

My father had a thing about giving me books as birthday presents that I wasn't yet grown-up enough to read. So that book just stood on the shelf – for a long time – with its tempting, evocative title. It was an important book, if only because of its title; and then it also seemed to hold out a promise for the future.

But why am I telling you all this in this context? I'm doing so because I think it's worth pushing the concept diaristic around a bit. It's a concept that for many good reasons comes up when you are dealing with this kind of picture-making. But maybe diary should be understood here even more literally than one would tend to at first. After all, a diary is per definition a writing-down of the topics of the day; in that sense it represents the remains of the day. But it's also a filter. In our diaries we write down the ***reflections*** prompted by the day's encounters with the world. So in that sense the diary is a day-to-day biography; it reaches further down into the personal than the day as such does; it brings out memories, and traces of language and emotions. It gives the day meaning. For the same reason it's interesting to read other people's diaries (you're not supposed to!) – for all their telegrammatic brevity and idiosyncratic privacy they are always also universally human documents.

If Michael Bevilacqua's constructions make complete sense to people who've never heard the same music as he has, or for that matter can't even begin to trace the migration of the icons from source to work, it's because they are diaristic in this broad sense. They are not only vehicles for a certain painterly effort to get everyday life into an artistic formula; they are (as Freud put it for the first time in his *Interpretation of Dreams*) constructed from the remains of the day; but the way they are constructed is overdetermined by the conscious and unconscious longings and drives of the personality, and they also deal with what came to you when you were eleven and too young to understand why it was important (like Joy Division's *New Dawn Fades* and a number of other musical allusions in the pictures, which refer to music from before Bevilacqua's teenage years). The imagery in these pictures are thus in a double sense the stuff that dreams are made of.

In short, I don't know whether Bevilacqua actually ever listened to the legendary German avant-garde rock group CAN – I guess he did, but it isn't all that important. I'm not even sure if I ever managed to read *The Kandy-Kolored Tangerine-Flake Streamline Baby Meets The Pump House Gang* all the way through, but it's *there* somewhere, and once every five years I get a chance to say all those words in that order (Wolfe's New Journalism from the sixties deals with California surfers, underground culture, art; it's hi-lo, diaristic and crossover, and if you like the paintings shown in this catalogue, you're sure to enjoy the read!).

Still life in the fast lane

In Michael Bevilacqua's compilations different forms of experience meld in a common formula. Elements taken from physical reality, fictive entities from widely different media such as film, video, print, neon signs and classical art all become painting, lose their own identity in the overall composition, while still to some extent keeping their reference to their origins. Roland Barthes called an early, brilliant essay on the classic still life "The World as Object". Objects were what there was, the world was, to quote the Danish author Klaus Rifbjerg, blissfully empty of anything else, and one uses what one has. A modern still life like those with which Bevilacqua works relates to a world of things and objects, but also a world of more intangible but no less *real* and meaningful signs. They cannot be read continuously like a rebus, but maybe as *bricolage*, that is as juxtapositions of parts from different meaning-universes that rub off on one another and together create a new one – or as examples of what the literary theorist Fredric Jameson has called *cognitive mapping*, the (post)modern individual's creative attempt at a consistent personal interface in an otherwise atomized culture.

The pictures then are *a kind of* diaries; they are built up of scraps from the artist's private life and an experiential horizon that is only partly congruent with that of the rest of us – symbol analysts or not. For it is important to note that the meaning-world with which we are confronted, despite everything, is neither random nor an attempt to catalogue things, but a quite specific cross-section of the icons of modernity. In this personal universe of the artist the stylized hair-do of the singer Björk from the cover of her CD *Homogenic* has taken over from the large Dutch cheese; the French rapper McSolaar's characteristic typography is substituted for the supposedly randomly scattered grapes. But the still life is still there: a cross-section of the world, arranged and composed and brought together on the painting's own aesthetic terms.

As if to give us a clue, Bevilacqua has most recently painted a series of pictures with clear references to the eccentric Italian painter Giorgio Morandi (1890-1964), who throughout his career refined a particularly mellow variety of the classic still life with bottles in particular set up in rows. The bottles are included in almost all Bevilacqua's latest pictures, and at the same time we note that he is now also working freehand without stencils or templates, and in the subdued areas of the colour scale mixed with black and white, which he normally skipped in the zeal of his early works. Look closely at the picture *Surface to Air*, which was painted last year. Here we find it all: the references to Pop Art, comic strips, children's books – and in the middle of it all Morandi's (now Bevilacqua's; after all the name means drinking water) bottles placed on the hood of one of the racing cars that started the whole business. But now all the spaces on the car are empty; where there were once stickers with logos, ads, pictures of all possible kinds (and on the real car in the exhibition miniatures and details from the painted pictorial universe you see on the walls), only the markings are now left. Zap, zap and cut. You have to be quick to follow an artist like Michael Bevilacqua. But you have to be quick slowly.

Requiem pour un twisteur. 1998

Michael Juul Holm (b. 1960) has been a critic and editor with a number of Danish papers and magazines since the early 80s, for six years a literary editor with Rosinante Publishers and since 2000 a curator with Louisiana and the museum's Head of Publications.

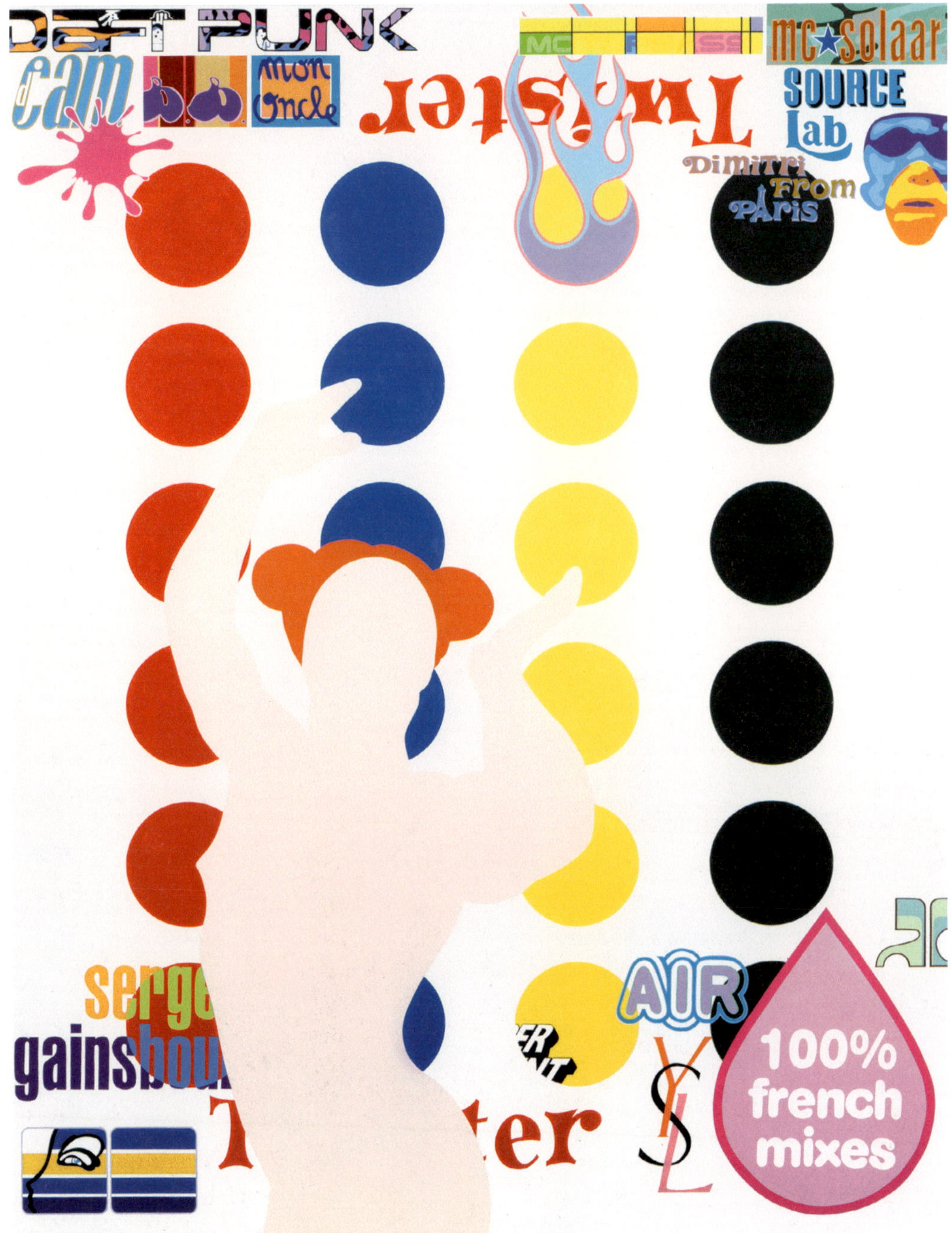
DAFT PUNK
mc★solaar
SOURCE
Lab
DiMiTRi From PARis
AIR
100% french mixes

Charade. 1998

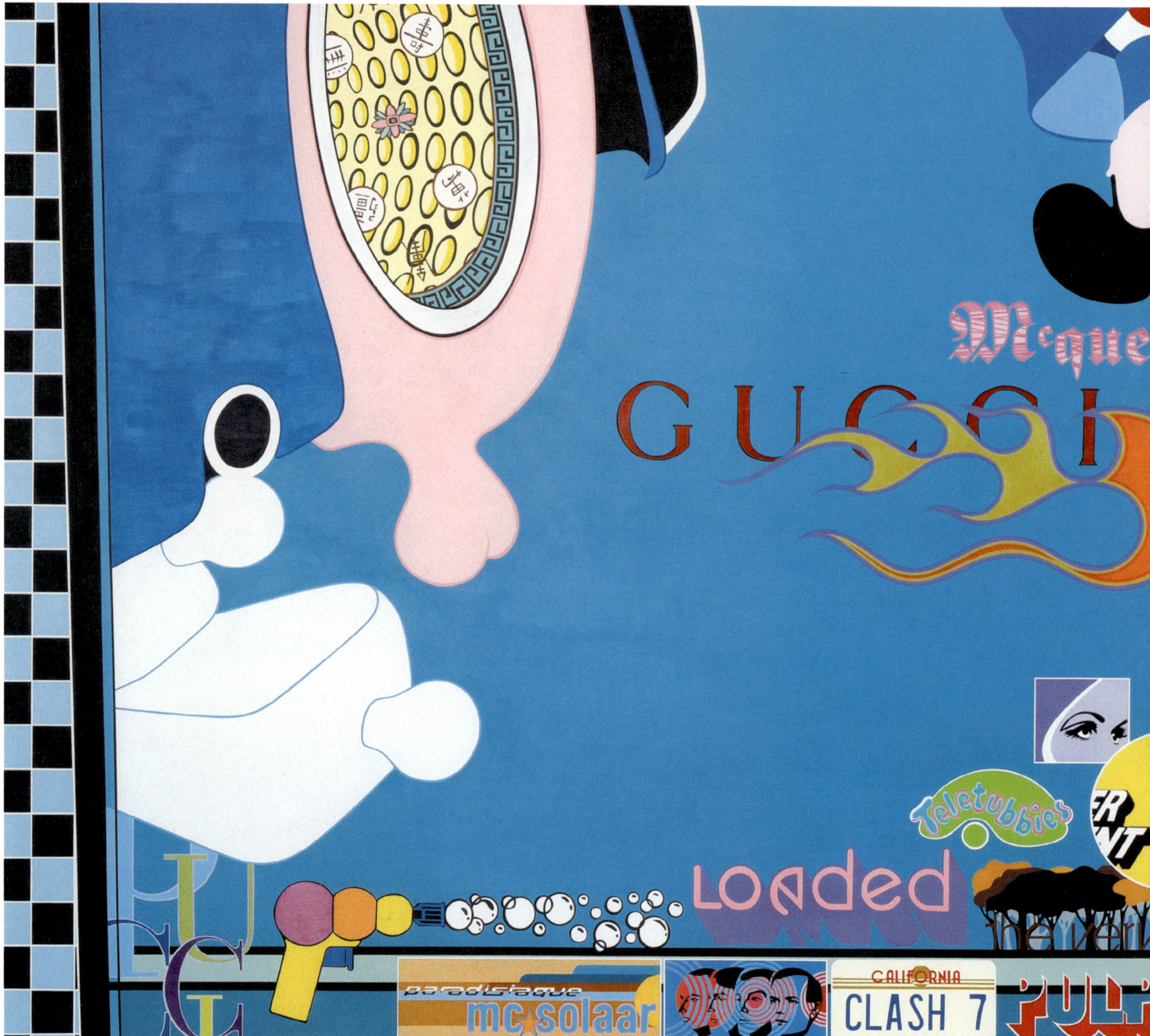

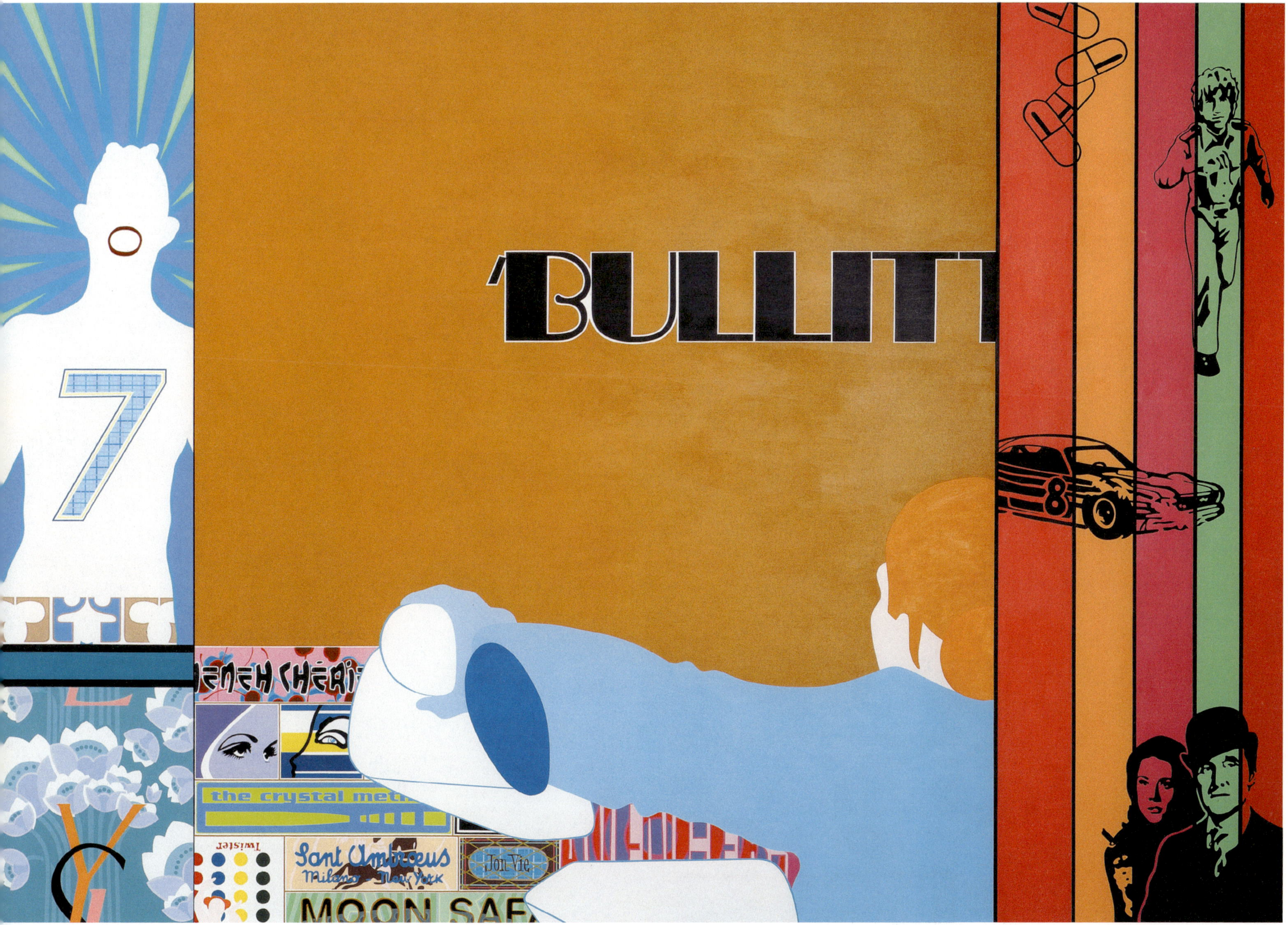
'BULLIT
7
the crystal meth
Sant Ambroeus
Milano New York
MOON SAF

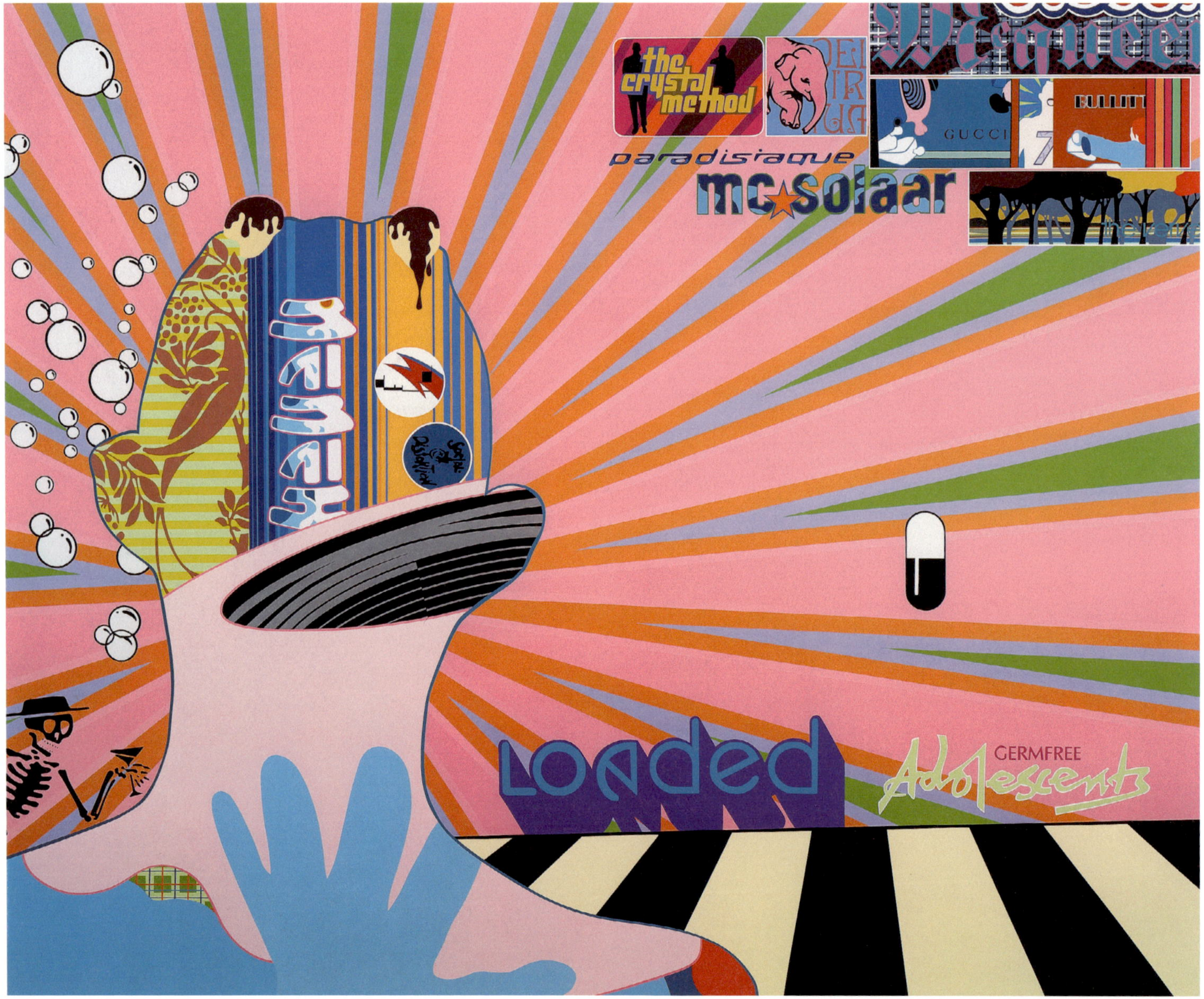
the crystal method
paradisiaque
mc solaar
GUCCI
BULLITT
Loaded
GERMFREE
Adolescents

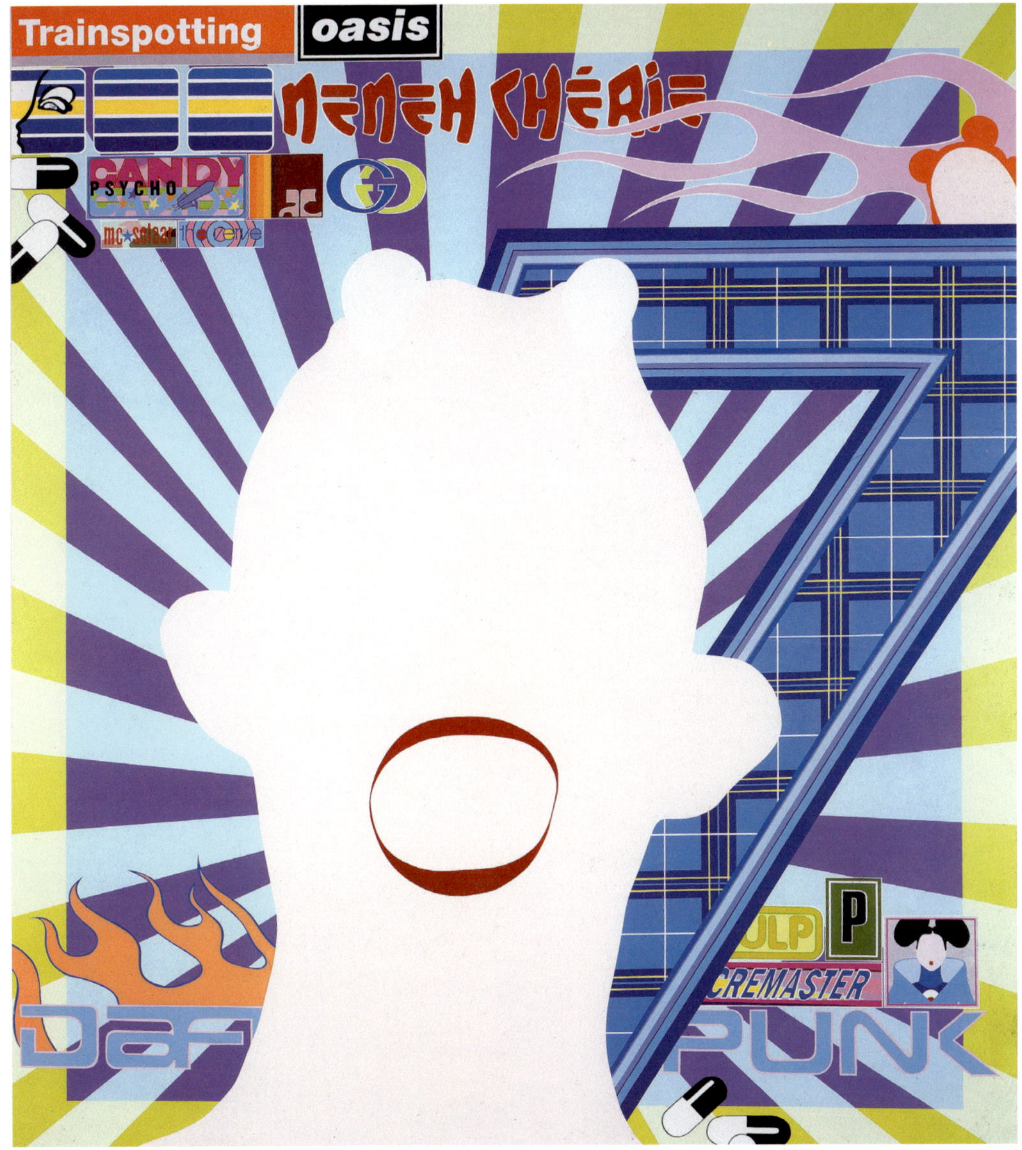

Screamadelica. 1997

< Humorous Pill. 1998

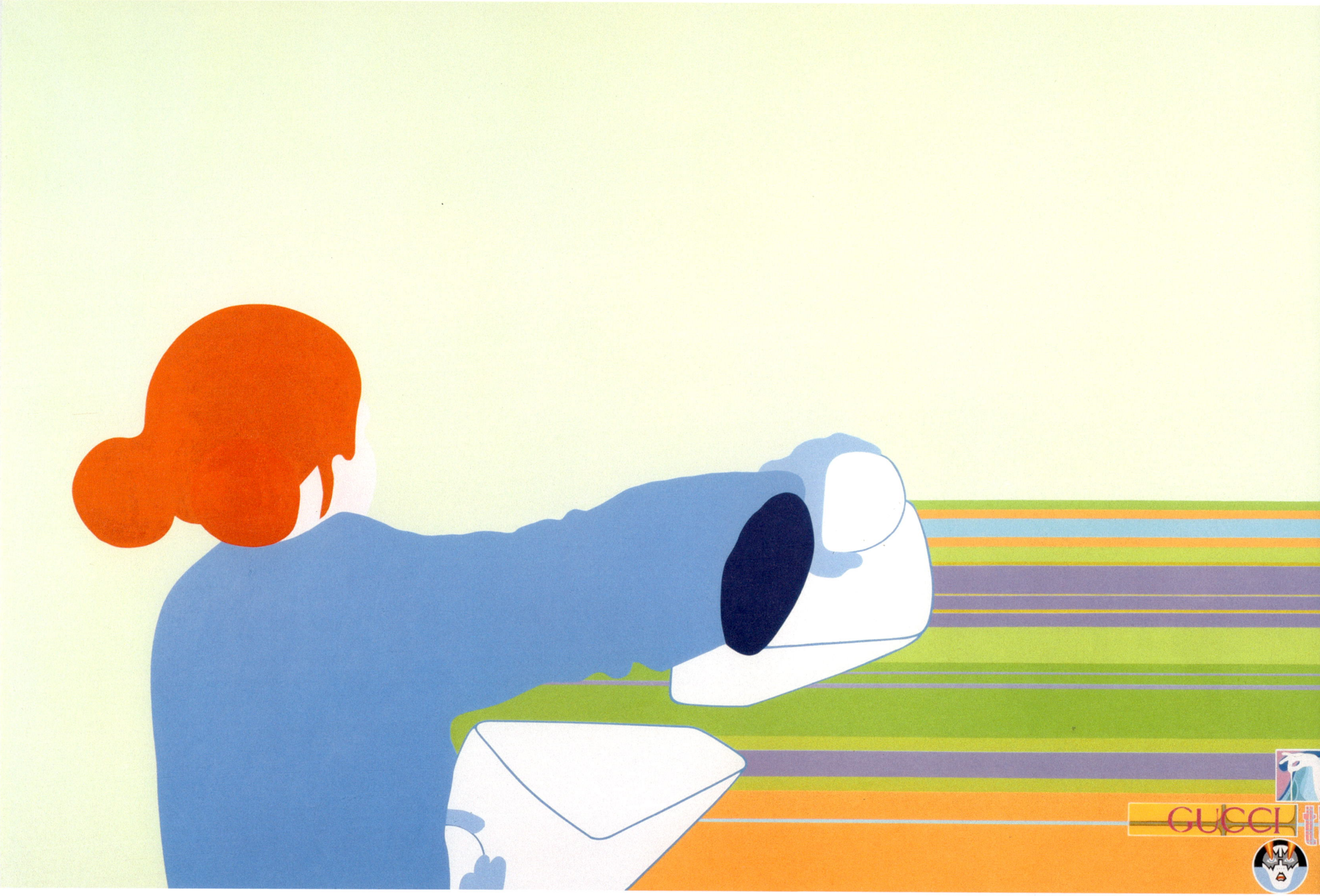
GUCCI

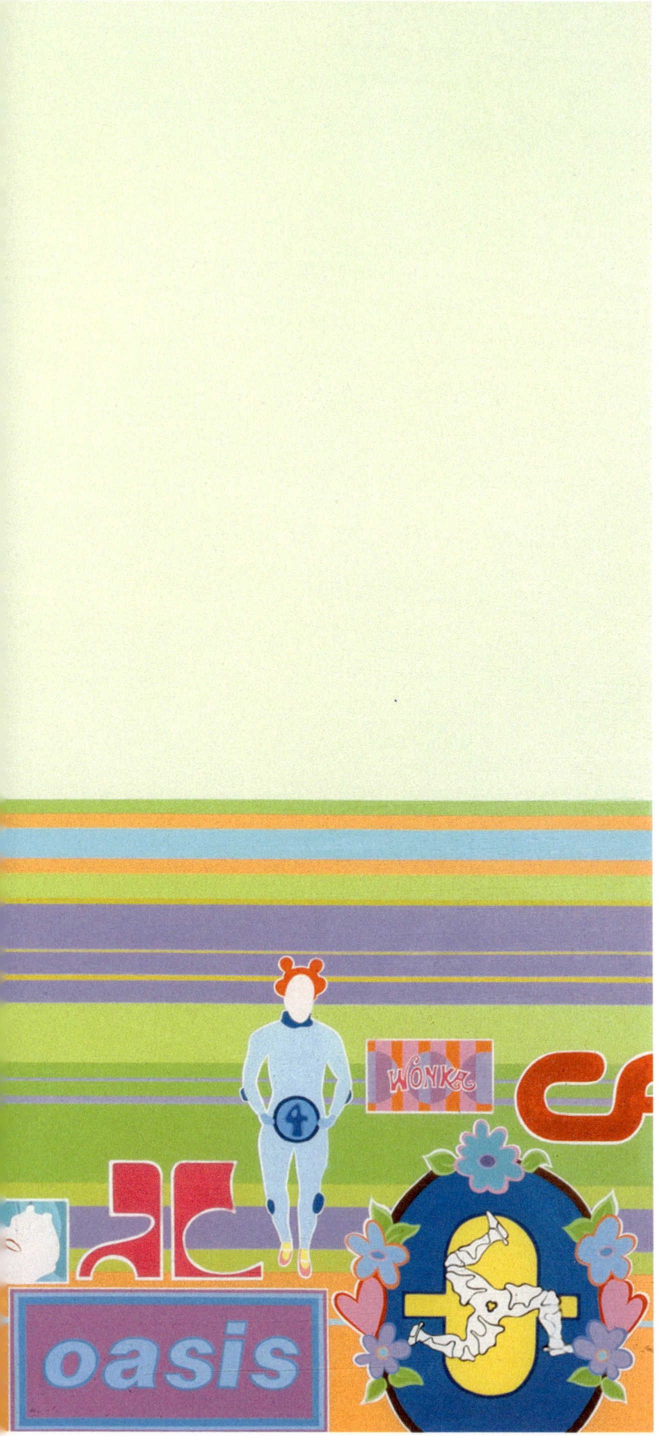

Life is Sweet. 1997

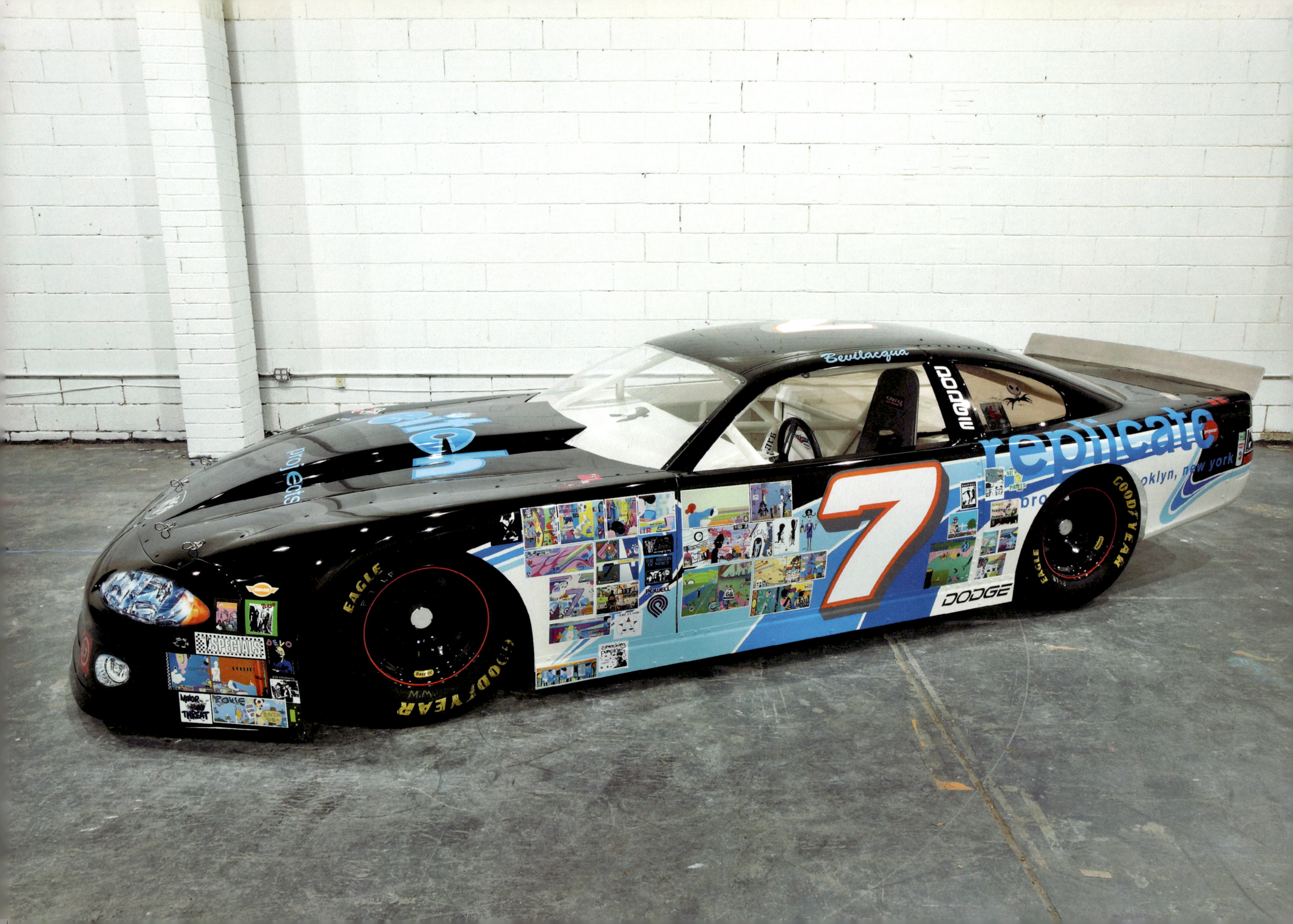

Bevilacqua
projects
replicate
7
DODGE
GOODYEAR
EAGLE
SPECIALS
DEVO
MINOR THREAT

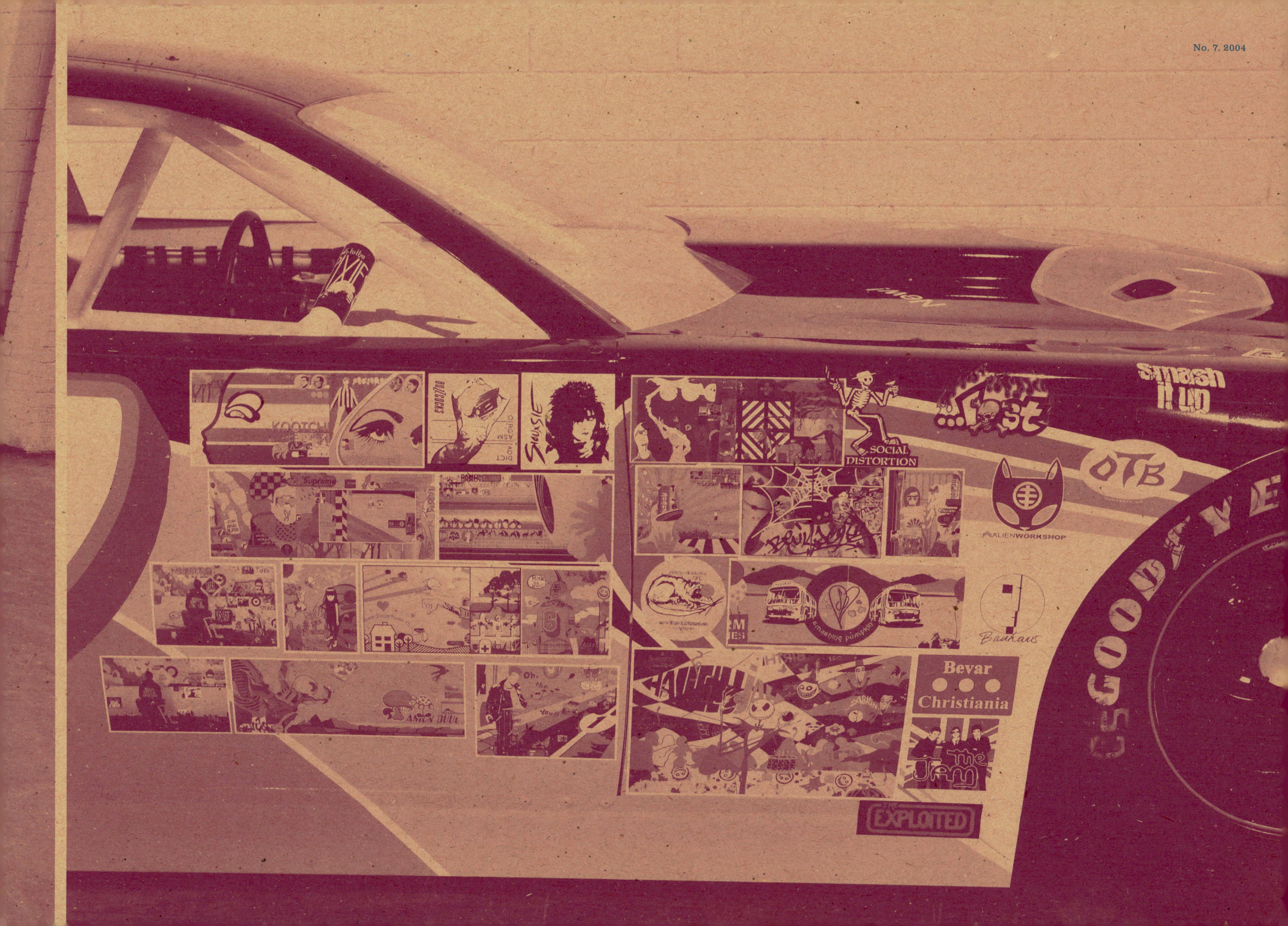
KOOTCH
Supreme
SIOUXSIE
SOCIAL DISTORTION
Smash it up
OTB
ALIENWORKSHOP
Bauhaus
Bevar Christiania
The Jam
EXPLOITED

BIOGRAPHY
MICHAEL BEVILACQUA

Born 1966
Lives and works in New York City

Public Collections
Louisiana, Humlebæk, Denmark
Astrup Fearnley Museum, Oslo, Norway
Deste Foundation, Athens, Greece
Dallas Museum of Art, Dallas, TX
Neuberger Berman LLC, New York
The Whitney Museum of American Art, New York
San Francisco Museum of Art, San Francisco, California
Orange County Museum of Art, California
Mitsuni Collection Tokyo, Japan

Solo Exhibitions

2005
Louisiana, Humlebæk, Denmark
Galleri Faurschou, Denmark, *Black Studio*
Deitch Projects, New York, *Surface to Air*
2004
Deitch Projects, New York, *Beyond and Back*
2003
Colette, Paris, *Vinyl Distraction*
Galleri Faurschou, Copenhagen, *Happy Nightmare Baby*
2002
Tomio Koyama Gallery, Tokyo, Japan
2001
Fredericks Freiser Gallery, New York City, *High-Speed Gardening*
1999
Jessica Fredericks Gallery, New York City, *Urban Hymns*
1997
Jessica Fredericks Gallery, New York City, *What Is It That Is The Worm Inside of You?*

Selected Group Exhibitions

2005
Palais de Tokyo, Paris, *Translation*
2004
Dakis Joannou Collection, Deste Foundation, Athens Greece
2002
Apex art c.p., New York, *The Passion of the Good Citizen* (brochure with illustration)
Kagan Martos Gallery, *The Dubrow Biennial*
2001
Deste Foundation, Centre for Contemporary Art, Athens Greece, *New Acquisitions from the Dakis Joannou Collection*
2000
Matthew Marks Gallery, New York City, *Drawings and Photographs*
Danese Gallery, New York, *Reconfiguration*
1999
Jessica Frederiks Gallery, New York City, *Pleasure Dome*
1998
Southhampton City Art Gallery/Arnolfini, Bristol/Oldham Art Gallery, GB, *Accelerator*
Matthew Marks Gallery and Pat Hearn Gallery, New York City, *Painting, Now and Forever* Part I
The Aldrich Museum of Contemporary Art, Ridgefield, CT, *Pop Surrealism* (catalogue, with illus.)
Castle Gallery, College of New Rochelle, New Rochelle, NY, *More Fake, More Real, Yet Even Closer* (curated by Robert Evren)
The New York Museum of Contemporary Art, New York City, *21st Anniversary Benefit Art Auction*
1997
The University of North Texas Art Gallery, Denton, TX, New American Talent: The Thirteenth Exhibition (chosen by Robert Storr, travelling/catalogue, with illus.)
1996
The Alternative Arts Fair, New York City, *The Most Important Thing in The World: Oasis vs. Blur and the Artists Who Rock* (curated by Bill Arning)
1995
The Phoenix Art Museum, Phoenix, AZ, *It's Only Rock and Roll* (curated David Rubin, cat, travelling)
1994
450 Broadway Gallery, New York City, *Page 5* (curated by Elizabeth Olbert)
1993
Dooley Le Capellaine Gallery, New York City, *Friendly (with Friends)*
1992
Vernon Space, Los Angeles, CA, *Industrial Heroes* (curated by Laura Howe)

LIST OF WORKS

Works in violet are in the Louisiana exhibition

Daytime Dilemma
(Dangers of Love), 2005
Acrylic on linen
24 x 18 inches / 61 x 46 cm
Collection Michael A. Nachman

Automotive Distraction II, 2004
Acrylic on linen
48 x 60 inches / 122 x 152 cm
Jessica and Andrew Freiser Collection

Beyond and Back, 2004
Acrylic on linen
72 x 96 inches / 183 x 244 cm
Collection of Jerry I. Speyer
Courtesy Deitch Projects

Black Studio, 2004
Acrylic on linen
72 x 240 inches / 183 x 610 cm
Neumann Family Collection

Drawing Under the Influence:
Geek USA, 2004
Acrylic on linen
72 x 192 inches / 183 x 488 cm
Private Collection

Highly Evolved, 2004
Acrylic on canvas
60 x 288 inches / 183 x 732 cm
Astrup Fearnley Collection, Oslo

Inside Looking Out, 2004
Acrylic on linen
72 x 108 / 183 x 274 cm
Private Collection, France
Courtesy Galleri Faurschou

The Mystery Spot, 2004
Acrylic on linen
96 x 72 inches / 244 x 183 cm
Courtesy Mitchell-Innes & Nash

Psypotica, 2004
Acrylic on linen
24 x 18 inches / 61 x 46 cm
Private Collection, Miami
Courtesy Galleri Faurschou

The Somnambulist, 2004
Acrylic on canvas
96 x 72 inches / 244 x 183 cm
Peter Bennedsen
Courtesy Galleri Faurschou

Surface to Air, 2004
Acrylic on linen
72 x 288 inches / 183 x 732 cm
Private Collection

Busy, Busy Sunny Day, 2003
Acrylic on linen
72 x 136 inches / 183 x 345 cm
Louisiana Museum of Modern Art, Humlebæk

Decline of Western Civilization, 2003
Acrylic on linen
48 x 120 inches / 122 x 305 cm
Private Collection, France
Courtesy Deitch Projects

Hallelujah: It's a Girl, 2003
Acrylic on linen
65 x 105 inches / 165 x 267 cm
Private Collection, Denmark
Courtesy Galleri Faurschou

New Dawn Fades, 2003
Acrylic on linen
36 x 96 inches / 92 x 244 cm
Private Collection, Denmark
Courtesy Galleri Faurschou

Gabba Gabba Hey, 2002
Acrylic on linen
36 x 96 inches / 91 x 244 cm
Private Collection, UK
Courtesy Galleri Faurschou

Happy Nightmare Baby, 2002
Acrylic on linen
37 x 46 inches / 94 x 117 cm
Neumann Family Collection

M1 – A1 (Teenage Wasteland), 2002
Acrylic on linen
48 x 72 inches / 123 x 183 cm
Collection of the Orange County Museum of Art,
purchased with funds provided by
The Neuberger Berman Foundation

Zero, 2002
Acrylic on canvas
72 x 96 inches / 183 x 244 cm
Bryan & Meredith Verona

Leave Home, 2001
Acrylic on canvas
78 x 60 inches / 198 x 152 cm
San Francisco Museum of Art,
purchased with funds by
The Neuberger Berman Foundation

High-Speed Gardening, 2000
Acrylic on canvas
102 x 126 inches / 259 x 320 cm
Dallas Museum of Art,
purchased with funds provided by
The Neuberger Berman Foundation

Picnic by the Motorway, 2000
Acrylic on canvas
60 x 156 inches / 152 x 396 cm
Neumann Family Collection

Atom Tan, 1999
Acrylic on canvas
36 x 43 inches / 76 x 213 cm
Neumann Family Collection

Shut Up, I'm Meditatin', 1999
Acrylic on canvas
74 x 156 inches / 188 x 396 cm
The Dakis Joannou Collection, Athens

Teen Spirit, 1999
Acrylic on canvas
43 x 36 inches / 109 x 91 cm
Collection of Norman Dubrow

Charade, 1998
Acrylic on canvas
60 x 152 inches / 152 x 386 cm
Neumann Family Collection

Do You Remember the First Time, 1998
Acrylic on canvas
72 x 60 inches / 183 x 152 cm
Neuberger Berman, A Lehman Brothers Company

Humorous Pill, 1998
Acrylic on canvas
60 x 72 inches / 152 x 183 cm
Private Collection

Requiem pour un twisteur, 1998
Acrylic on canvas
72 x 54 inches / 183 x 138 cm
Neumann Family Collection

Life Is Sweet, 1997
Acrylic on canvas
48 x 96 inches / 122 x 244 cm
Neumann Family Collection

Screamadelica, 1997
Acrylic on canvas
84 x 72 inches / 213 x 183 cm
Collection of Norman Dubrow

No. 7, 2004
Fibre glass, steel, plastic, race tires and paint
45 x 176 x 59 inches / 114 x 447 x 150 cm
Collection of the Artist
Courtesy Galleri Faurschou

This catalogue has been published on the occasion of the exhibition
LOUISIANA CONTEMPORARY: MICHAEL BEVILACQUA
June 18 – September 18, 2005
Curator: Poul Erik Tøjner
Coordinator: Anna-Maria Lund
Catalogue edited by Michael Juul Holm

Photo: Tom Powel, Farzad Owrang
Graphic design by Michael Jensen
Translations from the Danish by James Manley
Litho & print by Rosendahls Bogtrykkeri, Esbjerg
ISBN: 87-91607-12-4
Printed in Denmark 2005

NYKREDIT
Sponsor of Louisiana Contemporary 2005-2006
DONG
Main sponsor of Louisiana's exhibitions 2001-2005
REALDANIA FOUNDATION
Sponsor of Louisiana's architectural exhibitions 2005